Falling Through
the Cracks

Falling Through the Cracks

AIDS and the Urban Poor

Victor Ayala

SOCIAL CHANGE
PRESS

Ayala, Victor
Falling through the cracks : AIDS and the urban poor / Victor Ayala

Library of Congress Catalog Card Number: 95-70518
ISBN: 0-9644437-0-8

Copyeditor: Leslie Bernstein
Cover design: Gary Rogers
Interior design and composition: Guy J. Smith

Social Change Press, 38-15 Corporal Kennedy St., Bayside, NY 11361

Printed in Canada

10 9 8 7 6 5 4 3 2 1

Dedicated to

Stephen G. Catalano

and to

*the one hundred sixty-four people
with HIV/AIDS who trusted me
to tell their story*

Contents

Contents

FOREWORD

TO produce this book, Victor Ayala spent about ten years as a caseworker, a community liaison, and a public health educator in a hospital ward where gravely ill, indigent patients are treated for HIV-related illnesses. Oremus Hospital (a fictional name) is an immense public hospital in a borough of New York City that only the dead are said to know.

Ayala knows death well also. He knows even more about the peaks and valleys his patients will cross in their lonely journey through a fitful, often dehumanizing illness. But he does not think of himself in heroic terms. The counsel and comfort he offers to the patients whom the reader will meet in these pages are part of a silent crusade being carried out by thousands of dedicated medical and laypeople throughout the nation and the world.

In the face of a looming health care crisis for poor Americans, AIDS workers in public hospitals like this one devote their working hours and their productive years to caring for indigent AIDS patients. Many of the patients have personal histories that only Jesus himself could fathom and forgive, for the patients Ayala describes are perhaps the most woefully stigmatized people we can imagine. That says a great deal in a society known everywhere for its liberality in conferring stigma. I once asked

Victor how he decided on the fictitious names he uses to protect the patients' privacy. He told me that he names them after lesser-known saints.

At this writing there are presidential candidates who would demonstrate their rectitude by heaping calumny on these dying wraiths. The health care crisis they are manufacturing will make it even more difficult for the people Ayala describes to live out their short lives with anything approaching adequate care and a semblance of human dignity.

Indigent AIDS patients are at the very bottom rungs of status in our affluent society. The medical personnel Ayala works with are also among the most beleaguered in the field. Both conditions are due to the deadly illness they face, the fear it provokes, and, in the case of many patients, the extremely self-destructive lives that brought most of them to the edge of death at Oremus Hospital. They are suffering through the final months of a disease that is said to have all sorts of moral and economic meanings. But those meanings are not at issue here. The author's primary goal is to make the plight of the patients and the conditions in which their caregivers must work known in detail for whoever is open to a cry from the damned for aid and comfort.

Ayala develops no theory of AIDS and the very poor, offers no new concepts about AIDS treatment, coins no new sociological jargon in describing the world of indigent AIDS patients. In his desire to bring the reader into that world as it is experienced by patients and caregivers, he is "against interpretation" in the same way that Susan Sontag argued against affixing any theories or moral judgments or cultural messages either to cancer or to AIDS. "The age-old, seemingly inexorable process whereby diseases acquire meanings... is always worth challenging," she writes. Sontag also observes that AIDS evokes so much guilt and shame that "the effort to detach it from these meanings, these metaphors, seems particularly liberating, even consoling."[1] Sontag con-

cludes her argument against AIDS metaphors by plead-
ing with writers like Ayala to expose, criticize, and in
every way possible use up the excommunicating, stigmatizing imagery and metaphors of AIDS. Without calling explicit attention to his efforts on this front, Ayala
seeks to do battle against some of the worst stereotypes
and stigmatizing labels his patients are forced to endure.

Quite a few of the patients to whom Ayala intro-
duces us are not nice. Many are drug addicted, bitter
and angry, frightened and lonely. They are experiencing
social as well as physical death, and they themselves often come to feel that their illnesses are a form of retribu-
tion for their past sins. In bringing us to the bedsides of
dying and often wretched human beings, Ayala demands
that we witness the hospital situation as it is, with no
impression management or theoretical digressions to
blunt reality. Whatever meanings are to be had in the
experiences he describes result from our own realization
that no matter what we might think of the patients and
their behavior, they are being cared for by others who,
like the patients themselves, require our support and our
compassion. Failure to provide support for AIDS treatment targeted at very poor and troubled patients, once
one strips away the cynical fiscal arguments or the dema-
gogic moral ones, will only bring about more suffering,
guilt, and shame for all.

The patients who are described here as being literally scraped off the streets and brought to the emergency
room are suffering from, among other things, a shortage of adequate out-patient placements. Much of Ayala's
time is spent on the phone desperately trying to find
placements for men and women who are in the hospital
but will soon be disappearing into the streets. Intermi-
nable delays in finding placements put more people in
jeopardy, since they are not being treated in the streets
nor are the dangers they pose to others being addressed
at all adequately.

Surely Ayala would agree with Maxine Wolf, who

writes that "At early ACT UP NY meetings, it was usual
to hear people say: 'We don't want to help people die
anymore. We want to help people live.'"[2] For many in
New York and elsewhere, this desire translates into direct political action to confront the authorities and demand more resources for all aspects of the AIDS crisis.
Although many of the scenes in this book raise issues
about easing the death of indigent AIDS patients, Ayala's
larger agenda, and much of his work outside the hospital and the academy, is also political. He has been active
in AIDS-related political movements ever since the disease appeared. He is also among the activist pioneers in
that as a Puerto Rican New Yorker he recognized quite
early the need for more direct action among minority
people who were being exposed to HIV infection. His
work at Oremus Hospital is only one dimension of that
recognition. He has also been extremely active in the
leadership of the Brooklyn AIDS Task Force, for which
he has been honored in a citation by the president of the
Borough of Brooklyn.

The reader will not encounter many political activ-
ists among the rare visitors to the AIDS ward at Oremus
Hospital. Too many of these patients are people who
have remained outside the network of community-based
organizations that reach out to indigent populations.
Although there are successful models for such outreach,
they barely touch the lowest social niches. "It is easy to
point to the problem," Dennis Altman writes, but it is

> less clear to find easy solutions. When organiza-
> tions do seek to make major changes to accommo-
> date the new profile of the epidemic they risk alien-
> ating their original consistuency (and funders).[3]

There are simply not enough resources to show up in a
significant fashion in the scenes Ayala describes. This does
not mean that dedicated people are not working the
streets and alleys in the Oremus "catchment area" or that

volunteers from the community are not confronting the
authorities to demand more attention to the plight of
these patients. All this and more is occurring, but the
lack of evidence of any significant impact on the people
in this book merely signifies that more activism, more
resources, more dedication are urgently needed.

Scarce public funds are most likely to be directed
toward prevention of infection, rather than better palliative care and social resources outside the hospital (housing, counseling, home nursing). One obvious reason for
this is that public resources in most societies tend to go
to populations that are organized, can articulate their
needs, and show the promise that prevention efforts will
slow the spread of infection. Rev. Margaret R. Reinfeld,
director of education and international programs for the
American Foundation for AIDS Research, notes that "We
understand our task as changing social norms, not as
providing medical information." From years of experience with the Gay Men's Health Crisis, Rev. Reinfeld
has come to believe that the educator's job in confronting the AIDS crisis is to "change what the signs and sym-
bols of our sexual culture mean." If a man believes, for
example, that possession of condoms is somehow de-
meaning,

> a successful educational intervention will help him
> redefine that cultural meaning. He will leave the
> educational program believing that condom use
> means, 'I care about myself and my partner.'[4]

There is much wisdom in this approach, but impoverished and confused AIDS patients with debilitating symptoms of opportunistic dieseases often do not care at all
about themselves. Many have been unconsciously experi-
menting with various slow forms of suicide for some time.
Often, as we see in these pages, it is their lack of self-
respect and their inability to care for themselves that
makes them so difficult to reach through educational or

other interventions. This makes it all the more impera-
tive that their involvement with the hospital be one that
leads to new directions in their lives.

Ayala's description of the AIDS patients at Oremus
Hospital cannot be generalized to all hospitals treating
homeless and near-homeless AIDS patients. No doubt
there are hospitals where patients do not wait for long
hours on gurneys in noisy, dimly lit corridors. Surely there
are hospitals where AIDS patients with histories of IV
drug use are not moved so quickly through the revolv-
ing door from the emergency room to the streets. But
just as surely there are hospitals where the situation is
worse. The conditions experienced by indigent AIDS
patients at Oremus Hospital are by no means atypical,
especially as Medicaid funds and related programs are
slashed in state after state. By carefully documenting the
hospital careers of this patient population, Ayala makes
no claim for universality or statistical representativeness.
The strength of the ethnographic case study method he
uses is to present one such common but largely avoided
AIDS world in detail. Others may use his descriptive work
as a point of departure. No doubt, in time historians
seeking firsthand accounts of the AIDS pandemic will
find Ayala's work an invaluable primary source.

Much has been written about more affluent AIDS
patients and a great deal has been written about the
changing nature and course of HIV infection, but there
are few books like this one that actually present the disease from the viewpoint of its most reviled victims. In
bringing this book to completion, Victor Ayala has performed a second important service for his city and society. The first was, and is, his continuing service to people
with AIDS. For both of these vital services, and for his
continuing example, we are grateful to him.

William Kornblum
Chair, Center for Urban Studies,
City University of New York

Notes

1. Susan Sontag, *AIDS and its Metaphors* (New York: Farrar Straus Giroux, 1988), p. 94.

2. Maxine Wolf, "The AIDS Coalition to Unleash Power (ACT UP): A Direct Model of Community Research for AIDS Prevention," in Johannes P. Van Vugt, ed., *AIDS Prevention and Services: Community Based Research* (Westport, CT: Bergin and Garvey, 1994), p. 217.

3. Dennis Altman, *Power and Community: Organizational and Cultural Responses to AIDS* (London: Taylor and Francis, 1995), p. 77.

4. Margaret R. Reinfeld, "The Gay Men's Health Crisis: A Model for Community Based Intervention," in Van Vugt, *op. cit.*, p. 183.

PREFACE

THIS book addresses HIV/AIDS issues concerning the urban poor through their interactions with the health care system. Numerous factors are explored to highlight why this population is at high risk for the disease and probably will remain so. Limits on education regarding HIV transmission and AIDS, limited information sharing and dissemination, and limited access to health care and protective measures have helped trap this population in its high-risk status. Further, cultural upbringing shapes lifestyles to such an extent that it acts as a veil through which knowledge and information must penetrate.

Not only are the urban poor vulnerable to HIV infection and AIDS, but they have great difficulty negotiating proper medical care for their illnesses. The stigma of AIDS coupled with that of poverty, as perceived by health care workers, can affect their care and treatment. Unable to understand the illness, patients are unable to participate in their treatment--that is, to engage in effective discourse on treatment options, alternatives, and side effects.

To further complicate the situation, health care facilities are understaffed and some health care workers are untrained in the continuing complexities of AIDS care. In addition, shrinking state and city budgets have

resulted in the downsizing of hospitals and the elimination of local social service agencies.

This book attempts to correlate the urban poor to
society as a whole. It underscores their right to humane,
proper, and adequate medical treatment regardless of
lifestyle, social-class status, stigmas, and the perceptions
of health care professionals. It attempts to remind us of
our own mortality and our right to die with dignity.

I would like to thank the many dedicated health
care professionals who gave me their support during my
study. I am also indebted to William Kornblum, profes-
sor of sociology at the City University of New York, for
his encouragement and insight. Special thanks go to
Carolyn Smith of Social Change Press, whose professional
editing and expert advice brought this book to fruition.

Victor Ayala

INTRODUCTION

I N 1985 a friend, whom I will call Bill, was diagnosed as HIV-positive. Bill, a well-educated white
clergyman, was dedicated to serving God as the pastor of a local church. He lived alone in a solidly middle-
class neighborhood in Brooklyn, New York.

Not long after confiding in me about his HIV status, Bill developed what I would come to know as commonly experienced AIDS-related illnesses. From time to
time I helped him keep his medical appointments, visited him in the hospital, assisted with household chores,
and provided emotional support.

The most troubling thing about this experience was
the way Bill coped with his illness in near-isolation and
silence. He told only a few people about the diagnosis.
No one in his family or congregation was aware of the
nature of his illness or of his impending death. I could
not understand why he chose not to tell more people
about the situation. When he was hospitalized, he spent
much time alone and had only a few visitors. On many
occasions when I visited him I found him lying in his
own waste, confused and seemingly uninformed about
his medical condition or prognosis. After each of several
hospitalizations and discharges he returned home in a
weakened state, virtually unable to care for himself or
his two cats. Eventually a close friend moved into the

apartment to care for him.

In 1985 AIDS was a new medical dilemma. Little was known about effective prophylaxis. Treatment was not as multifocused as it is today. Life expectancy was no more than three years beyond the time of diagnosis. Bill was not even that fortunate. He died within six months.

There was no funeral, but a memorial service was held a month later in the church where he had served as pastor. Publicly, his death was attributed to cancer. The memorial was somber and predictable. There were few questions, no real attempt by members of the congregation to discover the real cause of Bill's death. Rather, there was silence. The silence of AIDS. I wondered how many other people were living and dying in the silence of AIDS.

Ten years have passed, and I have experienced the world of the AIDS patient from many perspectives. I continue to be profoundly struck by the silence that pervades the lives of people suffering from AIDS. Their inability to come to terms with their illness, the inability of friends and family members to come to terms with it, and the social stigma of AIDS all contribute to that silence.

In 1986, I took a part-time job with the New York City Department of Health's AIDS Hotline. As a telephone counselor I received an education about the nature of HIV infection and AIDS-related illnesses. I was responsible for providing information on the subject to anonymous callers. Beyond dispensing the latest news regarding the epidemic, I was exposed to the diverse social and sexual activities of the city's population. I was confronted with ignorance and fear in people who were concerned about being tested, people who had tested positive for HIV or were related to someone who was HIV-positive, and people who had developed AIDS-related illnesses. All kinds of people called the hotline: gay, straight, and bisexual, married and single, men and women, adolescents, young and mature adults, blacks, whites, Hispanics—all with varying degrees of curiosity, misinformation, concern, or panic.

One caller, Ana, telephoned me every Wednesday night. She was considering taking the HIV test because her husband, the father of her teenage children, had developed AIDS. The revelation that he had the disease had been accompanied by disclosure of his bisexuality. In addition to worrying about her health, she was coping with the issue of public disclosure. It was important to this middle-class Italian woman that her children, extended family, and neighbors be kept ignorant of the true nature of her spouse's illness. She lived in fear of contagion and of the stigma of AIDS. Yet she continued to care for her husband at home. She would lose him within the year and her eldest son the following year.

My conversations with Ana made me realize the anxiety that surrounds the issues of public disclosure and contagion. I soon found that fear is a dominant factor shaping the lives of people with AIDS.

As a counselor for the AIDS Hotline, I learned about the diverse conduits for transmission of the virus. I also learned how unwilling people are to change behaviors that put them at risk of contracting AIDS, even when they are aware of the risk. If members of the middle class were unable to make such changes, despite their access to information about the associated risks, what must the situation be for the poor, who generally lack access to information about AIDS?

A trip to Puerto Rico in the summer of 1987 gave me an opportunity to see the living conditions of poor people with AIDS. Clearly, this particular population had no access to health care. I began thinking about the poor in New York City, a city that offers state-of-the-art hospital-based medical care. I knew that if I took a closer look I would find gaps in health care, education, and political representation based on social class.

Once engaged in my study, I realized that indigent people with HIV and AIDS had no voice to speak for them. The media focused their AIDS coverage on white middle-class patients with access to high-quality health care. But there were no reports about the homeless men, women, and even children living in abandoned buildings and cardboard boxes. This community was suffering in silence. I vowed that through my study their voices would be heard.

Curiosity about the lives and circumstances of the urban poor suffering from AIDS prompted the choice of an ethnographic research methodology. To facilitate this approach I took a part-time position as a caseworker in a hospital. The job required that I provide direct, personal, one-to-one supportive counseling to AIDS patients. The location of the facility was such that the majority of the patients would be members of ethnic minority groups. My ethnicity and Spanish language skills would be especially useful.

Over a period of almost two years I investigated the prevailing conditions affecting poor AIDS patients in an urban hospital and their health service providers. The research was conducted in a New York City hospital, fictitiously referred to here as Oremus Hospital. I devoted most of my time to researching the care people received, their coping mechanisms, and available support.

There were usually about thirty patients in a ward; of these, twelve to fifteen were diagnosed as "full-blown" AIDS cases. My job involved counseling patients as fully as possible regarding their understanding of their diagnosis, the onset of AIDS-related symptoms, and the probability of their eventual discharge or demise. The methods used in my study included firsthand observation, formal and informal interviews, case histories, and field notes. The subjects participated voluntarily and were assured complete anonymity and confidentiality. This required that I use an alias for each individual I described or quoted. I devoted special attention to patients who entered the hospital via the emergency room and were ultimately transferred to one of the medical wards.

My research eventually involved 164 patients and their health care providers. Of the patients, 126 (77%) were male and 38 (23%) female. Sixty-eight (41%) were black males, 58 (35%) Hispanic males, 15 (9%) black females, 19 (12%) Hispanic females, and 4 (2%) white females. The mean age of the patients was a little over thirty-four years.

The African-American patients were of either native or West Indian origin; the Hispanic Americans were of Puerto Rican, Mexican, or Cuban ancestry. Most were adult males between the ages of eighteen and forty-five. All were living below or close to the poverty level as defined by the Census Bureau. They were, to varying degrees, uneducated, unskilled, unemployed, and often homeless.

Among the women patients, four (10%) believed that they had been infected with HIV by their sex partners. Twenty-six (68%) admitted to active intravenous drug use, and seven of them said that they participated in the sex trade to finance their drug use. Eighteen (47%) were homeless. The thirty-eight women had a total of twenty children; ten (26%) had more than one child. Most of the children were cared for by extended family members or were in foster care.

All of the patients had some experience with substance abuse. Twenty-four (15%) used cocaine; 25 (15%) admitted to using crack, the more addictive cocaine derivative; 118 (72%) indicated current or past intravenous drug use; and 45 (27%) admitted to alcohol addiction.

Intravenous drug use was the primary means by which the patients had contracted AIDS, accounting for 77% of the cases. Among the remaining cases, four had resulted from transmission from a heterosexual male to a female, ten from homosexual transmission, three from sexual trade, and eight from multiple-risk activity. Ten of the patients said that they did not know how they had contracted the disease.

Since the majority of the participants in the study

were intravenous drug users, it can be surmised with some confidence that they had contracted AIDS primarily via shared needles and secondarily via semen contact during sexual activity. The most common means of transmission was contact with infected blood during intravenous drug use. Some of the women who contracted the disease through sexual activity with an infected individual were engaged in the sex trade, in part to support a narcotic addiction; others traced their infection to unprotected sex with a friend or spouse who was an intravenous drug user. The three men in the multiple-risk category admitted to both intravenous drug or crack use and bisexual activity or paid sex with prostitutes. It thus was not possible to identify a single, definite cause of their infection.

Only ten (6%) of the patients described themselves as homosexual (four Latino and six black men). Half of this group openly discussed their homosexuality. They appeared to be relatively comfortable with this identity. The other half was less at ease with disclosure of their sexual preference and spoke of it only after several sessions. Despite the particular relevance of sexual preference for transmission of AIDS, this group tended to attribute their HIV-positive status or AIDS condition to intravenous drug use.

The majority of the patients studied (65%) lacked medical coverage. They received hospital-sponsored Medicaid, which remained in force only for the duration of their hospital stay. Fifty-three patients had Medicaid prior to admission to the hospital, and five had private medical insurance.

Eighty-seven (53%) of the patients studied died in the hospital; sixty-four (39%) were discharged. Thirteen (8%) left the hospital prematurely, against medical advice. The mean age at death for the male patients was 36.3 years; for the females, it was 34.4 years.

There is a strong correlation between lack of insurance and admission to the hospital via the emergency room. Only 10% of the participants in my study had been referred to the hospital by a physician—and in many of those cases the referral had been made by a health care provider at the hospital's satellite clinic.

Among the patients studied, fifty-eight (35%) had homes and could rely on some measure of family support; eleven (7%) had homes but had no family support. Sixty patients (37%) were homeless yet had some measure of family support. The remaining eighteen (11%) were homeless and had no family support.

The cases described in this book reveal a number of pathways to AIDS infection and a variety of ways of coping with the disease. Some of the patients were homeless individuals who had become infected through homosexual contact on the streets and in shelters; sexual deprivation, rather than homosexual identity, appears to be the reason for their exposure to the virus. There is much evidence in the social-scientific literature that indigence and sexual deprivation, regardless of an individual's social origins, tend to set traps that can themselves produce mental illness and disease. In such cases intervention—especially in the form of stable shelter, a job and income, and community attachments—can reverse much of the damage and enable the individual to move into the working class.

There are also cases, some of which will be described in this book, in which AIDS infection could be seen as a form of suicide and even, in a few instances, a form of aggression and murder. For many of the female patients, AIDS infection was a result of lives spent in the city's heroin and crack dens. Young women who trade sexual favors for drugs vastly increase their risk of contact with infected men. There is also an increased incidence of infection among women who are not themselves intravenous drug users but whose sexual partners may have been involved in the drug trade.

The urban poor are not usually reached or often persuaded by conventional educational messages about safe sex and other means of avoiding AIDS infection. In consequence, they are most likely to contract the disease. Once infected, they cannot afford quality care, are difficult to manage, and tend to receive substandard treatment. The further degradation that occurs as a result is demoralizing both to the patient and to the caregiver, further hindering treatment of these patients. The problems of inadequate care of poor AIDS patients thus are complex and self-perpetuating. Intensive, concerted efforts will be required if any progress is to be made toward alleviating those problems and perhaps helping some patients along the road to recovery or, at the very least, a more dignified death than they currently face in the AIDS wards of public hospitals.

This book portrays the experience of poor AIDS patients from their perspective, focusing on their interaction with the health care system. It explores the factors, such as lack of education and lack of access to health care, that tend to increase the level of risk faced by this population. It tries to show how vulnerable these patients are—their voices unheard, their fears unaddressed, their humanity unrecognized. It is my fervent belief that the urban poor have a right to proper and adequate medical treatment regardless of life-style, stigma, and the perceptions of health care providers.

1

Poverty, Social Isolation, and AIDS

AIDS is a complex infection that undermines the human immune system's ability to repel other diseases, thus leaving the body vulnerable to invasion by pathogenic organisms. The syndrome is linked to exposure to the human immunodeficiency virus (HIV). HIV can infect several types of human cells but shows a preference for the cells of the immune and central nervous systems, primarily cells with a particular type of receptor molecule or "port" on the cell membrane. Once attached, the virus must transform its genetic makeup to match the type encountered; it then inserts the copy into the host cell. The virus may remain dormant for some time, but it eventually becomes active and reprograms the host cell's DNA. This done, it reproduces within the cell, ultimately destroying the host cell. Before it dies, the host cell will have reproduced itself many times over, creating a multitude of new cells contaminated with the virus.

The virus's fondness for white blood cells, known as T-4 lymphocytes, is significant because these cells make up one of the immune system's primary lines of defense. The difficulty in fighting the virus lies in its ability to alter its external cell "armor," thereby becoming a variant or mutant that cannot be recognized by the body's natural antibodies or by artificial counteractive agents. Kaposi's sarcoma (a skin cancer) and pneumocystis Carinii pneumonia (PCP) are common opportunistic infections associated with AIDS. Others are toxoplasmosis, a type of brain inflammation; cytomegalovirus (CMV), a relatively common form of herpes simplex that causes inflammation in various tissues, including the retina, brain, and liver; herpes varicella zoster (chicken pox virus), which may cause shingles; tuberculosis; viral warts; chronic diarrhea (caused by Salmonella bacteria); cryptococcal meningitis; and thrush, a fungal infection of the mouth and throat caused by Candida. Some disorders, such as AIDS dementia complex (deterioration of cognitive, motor, and behavioral capacity), are caused primarily by HIV infection of the brain.

HIV is fragile and not easily transmitted. But upon infection it is found in all body fluids, both secretions and excretions. However, only blood, semen, vaginal secretions, and breast milk seem to be effective transmitters of the virus. The nature and transmission of the virus implies that it can be communicated from one person to another through exchange of these body fluids. Behaviors that seem most effective in transmitting HIV include intimate sexual contact, the exchange of used needles or syringes by intravenous drug users, and perinatal transmission of the virus from mother to child.

HIV exposure does not mean immediate experience of AIDS-related illnesses. It is not yet known precisely how much time must elapse between HIV exposure and the manifestation of those illnesses. Nevertheless, individuals who receive a positive test result are strongly advised to seek medical care. It is important to monitor their vital signs and initiate treatments that could prolong life and delay the onset of AIDS-related illnesses.

Infected individuals can also begin making conscious efforts to avoid infecting others. Initiation of "safe sex" practices and drug treatment, if applicable, are strongly advised. Here the medical evidence is unquestioned; the absence of symptoms does not preclude transmission of HIV.

The Incidence of AIDS

During the last ten years, while the numbers of people afflicted by AIDS rose, the profile of the "average" person with AIDS also changed. In the United States, AIDS patients initially were predominantly white, middle-class gay males. The infection spread among this population primarily through sexual intercourse. By the mid-1980s the profile had begun to change. The gay communities in major urban centers,

> preconditioned by many years of government indifference and supported by a healthy internal economy, sprang into action. The 'San Francisco Model' of volunteer health care organizations, counseling groups, and education programs was successful because the politically organized, empowered, and well-funded gay white male community could quickly come together.[1]

Although AIDS is still the leading cause of death among gay men between the ages of 25 and 44, the incidence of HIV infection is declining in this population.

African-Americans are among those hardest hit by the AIDS epidemic. The Centers for Disease Control estimates that 25% of all reported AIDS cases in the United States have been diagnosed in African-Americans. More than half of all women with AIDS—52%—are black.

Sixty-one percent of all babies born with AIDS are black, and black children account for 63% of all the children with AIDS. CDC statistics show that every two hours a black person dies of AIDS-related illnesses.

Similarly, the U.S. Census Bureau reports that Hispanic Americans account for only 10% of the U.S. population but for 15% of reported AIDS cases. Because a large number of individuals with AIDS are heterosexual male intravenous drug users, they put their sexual partners at risk. Hispanic women are eleven times more likely to become infected with the HIV than non-Hispanic women.

When these data are aggregated, one finds that whereas African-Americans and Hispanic-Americans represent 19% of the U.S. population, they account for 38% of AIDS cases. And this percentage is increasing rapidly. Intravenous drug use and heterosexual activity are the modes of transmission of 40% of AIDS cases among Hispanics and 45% of cases among blacks, but only 6% of cases among whites.

The quality of AIDS-related information is better now than it was in the early 1980s, and the educational response of certain communities, notably the gay community, has been significant. Yet the CDC estimates that 1 million Americans are infected by HIV, and CDC AIDS surveillance data indicate a total of 441,528 cases of AIDS in 1994. Of those cases, blacks account for 146,283 and Hispanics for 76,323.

Risk Factors in the Transmission of AIDS

Information about transmission and treatment is not having an equal impact throughout the population. This might explain why the incidence of AIDS is rising at a dramatic rate among certain socioeconomic subgroups. The spread of HIV infection has been virtually unchecked among black and Hispanic needle-sharers because AIDS education and prevention (counseling) have been targeted primarily toward the white middle-class population and have not adequately addressed the issues relevant to needle-sharers.

The incidence of AIDS in intravenous drug users (IVDUs) was first documented in 1984.[2] Needle-sharing has been reported to be a risk factor for these patients.[3] "Needle-sharing should be defined to include the sharing of syringes used for injection and possibly even the 'cookers' used for preparation of the drugs. Heroin and cocaine are by far the most commonly used injected drugs among IVDUs who have been exposed to the HIV, but the particular drug being injected does not appear to play an important part in the spread of the virus."[4]

There is evidence that women with AIDS deteriorate and die more quickly than their male counterparts. The differences in survival rates reflect the fact that poor women wait longer to get treatment because they lack financial access to the health care system and may be concerned that their children might be taken from them if they are diagnosed as HIV-infected. Also, women who use drugs are less likely to seek medical help for fear of being forced into a recovery program. They are, therefore, often diagnosed as having AIDS at a later stage of the disease. In addition, they may be in poorer health because of other factors such as malnutrition, poor hygiene, abuse, homelessness, and poverty. Among the patients I studied, most of the women died soon after entering the hospital because their HIV status was determined in conjunction with the onset of relatively advanced AIDS-related illnesses. Moreover, they were already in a state of physical decline because of minimal health care and the depredations of life on the streets.

It is also believed that AIDS may take a different course in women than in men, perhaps because of hormonal differences. Moreover, pregnancy weakens the immune system, making women more susceptible to infection.

Many infected persons have lost their jobs, homes, and insurance coverage. Although Medicaid provides some assistance, funding is limited. Some pregnant women who have tested positive for the virus choose to terminate the pregnancy. But without Medicaid many poor women have no such option. Some women visit doctor after doctor in a vain attempt to secure an abortion. Most are unsuccessful and are forced to carry the child to term. Generally, all women labeled "high-risk" face the same kind of discrimination or potential problems, whether or not they have the virus.

Falling Through the Cracks

AIDS is especially prevalent among the poor—in particular, the permanently impoverished residents of the nation's inner cities. This population includes the passive poor (usually long-term welfare recipients); the hostile poor (e.g., agressive criminals), who are allegedly responsible for much violent inner-city crime; hustlers living off the underground economy; and the traumatized poor—substance abusers, the homeless, and the mentally ill. In demographic terms, the majority of the urban poor are female-headed, welfare-dependent families and single, young, unemployed ethnic minority males. On the East Coast they are concentrated in Boston, New York, Philadelphia, and Washington, D.C.

Many people living marginal lives on the bottom rungs of society's economic ladder suffer grinding poverty and despair. Their plight is both a cause and an effect of America's most persistent social problems. They experience disproportionately high rates of teenage pregnancy, single-parent households, chronic unemployment, crime, drug abuse, welfare dependency, and homelessness. Isolation and concentration worsen the frustration, passivity, and hostility that mark the lives of ghetto dwellers.

In the mid-1980s health care analysts and urban sociologists became aware that low-income and minority people constituted the fastest-growing proportion of the population of persons afflicted by AIDS. Black and Hispanic community leaders were especially alarmed, since their communities already experienced disproportionately high rates of joblessness, teenage pregnancy, female-headed households, welfare dependency, crime, and incarceration. As just noted, urban ghetto neighborhoods were becoming economically and socially isolated; social scientists thus began to fear that this isolation would facilitate the catastrophic spread of an incurable disease through an already severely disadvantaged population.

In a medical crisis such as the AIDS epidemic, the availability of current, factual information is essential if large numbers of people are to avoid infection or cope appropriately with the disease. The urban poor, however, are unlikely to encounter this vitally important information. There have been educational and public relations campaigns, both national and grassroots in scope, to alert poor inner-city minority populations to the dangers of AIDS and the precautions necessary to inhibit the spread of the disease in their communities. Despite these efforts, it is clear that the epidemic is taking a greater toll among these groups than in the population as a whole.

The spread of AIDS among the nation's poorest people severely strains the capacity of political and social-welfare institutions. While the world awaits a cure for AIDS, there is general agreement that the only effective routes to prevention hinge on mass education and, some will assert, more draconian measures such as contact notification.[5] Recent evidence indicates that more affluent and educated citizens have modified their behavior and are experiencing decreasing rates of infection, especially outside major metropolitan regions. In contrast, low-income members of minority groups living in areas characterized by high rates of intravenous drug and crack use are among the highest-risk groups in the nation.

This book is concerned with AIDS patients from one of the nation's poorest urban neighborhoods. This population suffers from the stigma associated with low socioeconomic status. The patients spoke of their frustration with unemployment and the difficulty of trying to cope from day to day. Their family lives, many long since fractured or broken, had been plagued by domestic violence, sexual abuse, and absentee parents. Their sense of personal failure, coupled with the lack of economic and social opportunities, had led to alcohol abuse, drug use, reliance on public assistance, or homelessness. In these contexts they were exposed to HIV, and many eventually developed the AIDS-related illnesses that brought them to the emergency room of a public hospital.

Notes

1. Angela Mitchell, "AIDS: We Are Not Immune," *Emerge: Our Voice in Today's World*, November 1990, p. 34.

2. R. M. Selik, H. Haverkos, and J. Curran, "Acquired Immune Deficiency Syndrome (AIDS) Trends in the United States, 1978–1992," *American Journal of Medicine*, 76 (1984), pp. 493–500.

3. Ibid.

4. H. Cohen, M. Marmor, and D. Des Jarlais, *Behavioral Risk Factors for HTLV-III/LAV Seropositivity Among Intravenous Drug Abusers,* paper presented at the International Conference on AIDS, Atlanta, Georgia, April 14–17, 1985.

5. Ronald Bayer, *Private Acts, Social Consequences* (New York: Free Press, 1989).

2
Entering the Hospital

ON a sweltering Friday evening the Emergency Medical Services Unit at Oremus Hospital in New York City receives an anonymous call reporting a motionless man lying in an abandoned car several blocks away. Paramedics are dispatched to a street lined with gutted buildings, broken glass, and abandoned, stripped vehicles. They find a Hispanic adult male in a semiconscious state and in urgent need of medical attention.

Miguel, as he will be called here,* is transported to the emergency room (ER). As the team arrives, the ER is filled to capacity. Men with cut arms and heads are waiting for attention. Children suffering from asthma attacks are anxiously clutching their mothers. Because his feeble vital signs indicate that he may be close to death, Miguel is given immediate attention by harried doctors. They stabilize his heartbeat and breathing. The physicians rule out seizure disorder and drug overdose as possible causes of the medical crisis. Further care is limited for now because Miguel lacks personal identification and no family members are present. For administrative purposes he is assigned a number and a chart is prepared listing him as "name unknown." Still semicon-

---

*All patients' names have been changed to maintain confidentiality.

scious, he is left on a stretcher in an adjacent hallway with ten other patients in similar states, all awaiting hospital beds.

Esperanza is another of the patients lying on gurneys outside Oremus's ER on this hot August night. Earlier that afternoon she was brought to the ER by her mother. For several days she has had severe headaches and high fevers, and today she is unable to walk. She has been in poor health for the past year. Two years previously a Department of Health counselor arranged for tests that showed that Esperanza is HIV-positive. Despite the gravity of this news, she was told that there was nothing she could do until she actually became ill. She received no treatment or advice about what to expect in the future. Now she is diagnosed as suffering from cryptococcal meningitis. Her fever is extremely high. Without immediate medical care she could easily die, despite her relative youth.

Delores, a forty-three-year-old black woman, has been living in a public shelter. During the past two months she has lost twenty-five pounds. Over the past several days she has suffered a 104-degree fever, vomiting, and diarrhea. Earlier on this same August day a concerned staff member "dragged" her to the ER. There she was examined by the attending doctors, who were able to conduct numerous tests to determine her medical condition. The results, however, serve only to rule out several possible diagnoses; they are insufficient to identify the precise disorder from which she is suffering. Now she waits on a gurney for additional information about her illness so that she can be either released or admitted.

Another patient waiting in the hallway is Canute, a twenty-nine-year-old Hispanic male who was brought to the ER by a community medical center's ambulance service. Like Miguel, he was found lying near death on the street not far from the community health clinic. Since Canute is unconscious, it is fortunate that the ER staff remembers that he was there three days earlier, suffering from HIV-related illnesses. These are now complicated by a heroin/cocaine overdose, shortness of breath, and a high fever.

The mood of the ER today is no different than usual. As always, it is extremely stressed, especially on a Friday night. Obviously, the patients are not there by choice. Their urgent medical conditions have been precipitated by accidents, violence, or long-ignored physical problems. The room is filled to capacity with patients who for the most part do not have regular doctors and receive medical attention only in emergency situations, even if the symptoms do not actually constitute an emergency.

After a wait that may vary from a few minutes to two days, depending on staff availability, the patient, if conscious, or an accompanying person is interviewed by ER intake personnel. At this point formal medical record-keeping begins. The purpose of this interview, the first of many, is to obtain general personal and demographic information, including original symptoms, name, address, employment history, insurance coverage, and next of kin. For the unconscious Canute or Miguel the staff will do the best they can to determine the cause of the condition and take steps to revive the patient so that more information can be gleaned if possible.

Again depending on the number of cases and staff availability, the patients wait for some time to see a physician. Those who were escorted by paramedics now wait alone. Those who were brought in by friends, family members, or others are sometimes, but not always, accompanied by those individuals during this interval. Upon the physician's arrival, intake data are confirmed and a physical examination is conducted. The examination encompasses assessment of the patient's chief physical complaints and his or her psychological, social, and medical background. Clothes and other possessions are relinquished and replaced by a hospital gown and a plastic identification bracelet. A doctor decides whether or not the patient will be transferred from the ER and admitted for care in a medical ward. This decision is based on a preliminary diagnosis.

Next, a process of stabilization and treatment is developed. Eventually, depending on the availability of beds, the patient is transferred to a room in a medical unit, where a new set of doctors, nurses, and social workers reassess his or her state of health and personal history. The purpose of this reassessment is the creation of records for managerial, financial (reimbursement), and educational purposes. An effort is made to gauge the patient's understanding of the condition and the diagnosis and to elicit his or her cooperation in the treatment process. But in order for substantive treatment to begin, the patient must be assigned a bed in the medical ward.

It is not uncommon for people to wait days for a bed. In Miguel's case, for example, an ER social worker attempted an interview, but Miguel was unable to answer the questions. Forty-eight hours later he remained unconscious and was transferred to the medical ward. There too, the general intake worker was unable to learn his name or any other personal information. In one of the ward's twenty-eight private rooms, his clothes were removed and discarded. Several hours later his condition improved and he was able to talk to the medical ward staff. A more thorough examination was then carried out that enabled the staff to rule out pneumocystis Carinii pneumonia (PCP), tuberculosis, and anemia.

Most indigent AIDS patients arrive at the hospital in a state requiring emergency assistance. If they are alert, they are distressed, confused, and afraid; sometimes bewildered or incoherent; and generally in pain. Whatever is happening to their bodies is beyond their control. Characteristically, long-untreated conditions have become unmanageable to the point of incapacitation. They want the problem "fixed" as soon as possible so that they can return to their normal routine.

Prior to their arrival at the ER, the patients were autonomous. Now they express discomfort with their unfamiliar environment, the strange hospital procedures, and the partially unrecognizable jargon used by hospital personnel. They are reluctant to release personal information that may reveal illegal practices (drug abuse, prostitution) or unconventional life-styles (homosexuality, homelessness). All this serves to inhibit them at a time when frankness and openness would be most beneficial.

The Hospital

Oremus Hospital (not its real name) is of recent construction and occupies an area approximately the size of three city blocks. The ethnicity of the population in the surrounding neighborhood is similar to that of the patients studied. Many parts of the neighborhood consist of abandoned buildings, shattered storefronts, and littered alleys. Construction of a housing project for low-income families is under way.

In many ways the quality of care AIDS patients receive is determined by the hospital's physical structure and management policies. The design of the hospital emphasizes efficient delivery of care and maintenance services. The facility operates around the clock every day of the year. Its policy is to provide care without regard to race, creed, color, or financial resources. On its staff are more than 2,400 professionals, supplemented by an extensive and varied pool of volunteers with diverse responsibilities. Turnover and absenteeism are major problems, especially in the emergency room, nursing, and social services units.

Oremus Hospital has approximately 600 certified beds and admits more than 20,000 patients per year. The hospital is fully accredited by the Joint Commission on Accreditation of Health Care Organizations and is approved for internship and residency training by the Accreditation Council on Graduate Medical Education. Its house staff is composed of more than 130 interns, residents, and fellows distributed throughout the departments of medicine, surgery, pediatrics, and oral surgery.

The hospital's inpatient services include units in general medical and surgical specialties, pediatrics, alternative care, rehabilitation medicine, medical and surgical intensive care units, and coronary care. It also has a mental health department with six inpatient units, alcohol and drug detoxification units, and a psychiatric emergency department. Outpatient services include adult mental health, alcoholism, and child/adolescent mental health services.

Oremus Hospital serves a diverse community of approximately 500,000, the majority of whom are African-American, Caribbean-American, and Hispanic. A significant portion of the community is made up of recent arrivals from impoverished third-world countries. Thirty-three percent of its inhabitants live below the federal poverty level, making this community a socioeconomically depressed area. The median annual income is $13,382 for individuals under age sixty-five, and only $8,700 for householders age sixty-five and over, compared to $27,700 and $12,500, respectively, for New York City as a whole. More than three-quarters of the hospital's revenue comes from Medicaid.

As of this writing, Oremus and other public hospitals that treat a disproportionate number of the urban poor, among whom are many AIDS patients, will receive significant cuts in staff and in the programs that those who counsel AIDS patients rely on. If anything, the situations and cases described here will worsen in coming years.

Hospital Admission Policies

As with any other illness, there exists a model for the delivery of health care services to AIDS patients. It includes examination, diagnosis, determination of treatment strategy and methods, nutrition, discharge, and aftercare or outpatient services. The reader will learn throughout this book how effective implementation of this model is undermined by personnel and material shortages as well as by counterproductive attitudes on the part of both patients and staff members.

Special teams are available to serve every aspect of a patient's needs. There is a strong link between the hospital's satellite clinics and its inpatient services. In the neighborhood are a few clinics equipped to deal with HIV-positive individuals and ambulatory persons with AIDS. But illiteracy and resistance to care guidelines are major difficulties. Patients generally do not practice preventive medicine and do not have personal physicians or health insurance. Most often the AIDS patient's primary exposure to medical treatment takes place in the emergency room.

Hospital administrators have long-established procedures for admission of patients. These procedures are designed to identify medical needs, gauge the facility's ability to provide relevant services, and determine how those services will be delivered. In this way the administration maximizes the efficiency with which care is provided and minimizes financial costs and the demands placed on the staff, while optimizing the patients' chances of recovery.

Patients are admitted to Oremus Hospital in two ways. The first is by request of a resident physician who is the personal doctor of a specific patient. This is not common in the case of poor AIDS patients. It is, however, common for such patients to be admitted by way of the second alternative: the emergency room. Indeed, the ER is the usual entry point for people experiencing life-threatening conditions. Medical attention is sought at this time because the person has become incapacitated by symptoms such as high fever, persistent vomiting, extreme pain, or unconsciousness.

Canute, Dolores, Esperanza, and Miguel are typical patients in this regard. Although there are important differences in their cases, just as each person suffering from AIDS-related illnesses has a unique story to tell, in certain ways each is typical of the brutal plight of the indigent AIDS patient in a public hospital.

When Miguel and Canute were being literally scraped off the streets by paramedics, no one questioned the order that care should be given. Somewhere in the state capital or in Washington there was a task force debating how to reduce the burden placed on society by such patients. But in the ER there is no philosophical debate when help is needed. As Dolores rants incoherently through her fever about her children and the wrong she has done them, no doctor or nurse ever wonders if it would be just as well to let her go out in the street to die. The caseworkers at the shelter who half-carried Dolores across the city to the hospital never thought about just letting her die in a corner. As each of these patients waits for the process of hospital admission to continue, there is never a moment when anyone questions whether care should be given at all. The medical norms about the sacredness of life run deep in the hospital system.

The Medical Record

Enforcement of the hospital's care policy is documented by way of the medical record, which is a major part of the care process. All personal and health-related information gathered by the doctors, nurses, social workers, and other health care providers becomes part of this permanent record. It is the primary means of communication among hospital personnel concerning individual cases, since it includes lab test results, daily vital signs, physician's instructions, and medication types and dosages. Cryptic comments and sentence fragments are used in recording pertinent information in order to minimize the length of the record. Technical medical terminology is used to define and describe the patient's condition and progress.

The "progress note" section of the record chronicles the specific actions taken by the staff in relation to the patient. Because of the number and variety of individuals who contribute to these records, the report must be standardized. A kind of boilerplate language is used— for example, "Patient is a 35-year-old, single, Hispanic male with history of IVDU; in good health until three days ago. Complains about generalized body aches and vomiting 3X day and fever."

Current medical records are inventoried at the nurses' station located in each medical ward. At Oremus Hospital there are two wards on each floor. Here doctors, social workers, and nurses converge to record relevant data on patient care and social interactions between patient and staff. Each caregiver is introduced to the case by way of the medical record.

Great emphasis is placed on documentation. All health care providers are required to note every instance of contact with each patient. Hospital administrators and government officials rely heavily on these documents to assess the extent and quality of medical attention provided by the hospital. As one physician stated, "Medical and health-related staff spend about 70% of their time treating the medical record and 30% of their time treating the patient."

The social workers are concerned with the patients' psychosocial histories, their understanding of their diagnoses, possible referrals to public agencies, and appropriate discharge planning. They are concerned that people with AIDS who are in need of services be reported to the Division of AIDS Services of the city's Human Resources Administration in a timely fashion (i.e., within 72 hours). They also try to ensure that necessary assessment forms are completed, AIDS support groups engaged, and family members actively sought and involved in the case. Finally, they attempt to develop a specific hospital discharge plan.

The medical record has effects beyond its immediate purpose. The subjective impression formed by the content, language, and detail used to complete the report affects the manner in which a patient is approached. The very mention of antisocial or deviant behavior patterns signals staff members in a way that may affect interactions with the patient and the quality of care provided. Documents including comments such as "Patient is an active drug abuser...homosexual male...homeless...prostitute" conjure up stereotypical and stigmatizing images in the minds of staff members. Such patients are distinguished from the "good" patients, who are considered to be ill through no fault of their own.

Testing and Diagnosis

If the hospital is to fulfill its mission as a medical service provider, the staff must determine the cause and nature of the illnesses afflicting those who come to it for assistance. When this information is obtained, the focus of the staff's interaction with the patient shifts to treatment or cure. It behooves the doctors to prescribe expeditious therapies so as to minimize costs and discharge patients as quickly as possible.

When the ER examination indicates that hospitalization is necessary, the patient is referred to a medical unit. Symptoms are treated, but the information obtained in the ER exam must be refined before an appropriate care plan can be developed. The social and personal information obtained during the ER interview may suggest that the patient has engaged in "at risk" behavior. In such cases the patient is introduced to a nurse clinician, who obtains more specific information about the patient's social activities, HIV status, and AIDS awareness. The issue of confidentiality is discussed. A consent form is signed before HIV antibody tests are administered. A blood sample is taken and the sample sent to an external laboratory for processing. Patients who agree to take the test remain in the medical ward for treatment of the symptoms observed in the ER.

It takes two to three weeks to obtain HIV test results. In the meantime the staff can do little more than treat symptoms and make the patient comfortable. If the condition is not critical, patients may be permitted to check out of the hospital if they wish. They are instructed to rest and take the prescribed medication and are referred to an outpatient clinic for medical follow-up.

When the test results are returned, the HIV counselor delivers the results to the patients who are still in the hospital and arranges for appointments for those who have been discharged. Patients with positive results are referred for medical follow-up. Patients with negative results are given information concerning transmission of the virus.

Some patients are already aware of their HIV status and inform the staff accordingly. The staff knows that the current symptoms may represent the development of HIV-related illnesses. Therapies are identified and initiated. If the appropriate resources are available, the staff begins treatment of the specific disease.

In the absence of test results, for treatment purposes the hospital considers a patient to have AIDS if two or more HIV-related infections are manifest and there is a low CD4 count. In Miguel's case the infectious disease specialist discusses the results of a bronchoscopy with him. The diagnosis, pneumocystis Carinii pneumonia, requires three weeks of specialized treatment. In addition, he explains, the drug known as AZT may slow further infection and prolong Miguel's life. But the terminology used by the doctor is too complex and formal; Miguel cannot understand it.

The social work team provides counseling and identifies potential social services. Homeless patients are referred to the Division of AIDS Services of the Human Resources Administration to obtain residential referrals, financial assistance, supportive psychosocial counseling, and if necessary, outpatient therapies or long-term care. The Division of AIDS Services will provide housing if the hospital social worker confirms that the patient is homeless and the medical staff provides test evidence of HIV-related illnesses. Generally, housing consists of single-room-occupancy hotels or private or group homes anywhere in the municipality. The number of such accommodations is limited, and patients may have to wait several weeks or months for appropriate housing. In the meantime the patient must stay in the hospital, since internal policy and municipal law prohibit the release of a homeless AIDS patient.

Financial assistance is in the form of Supplemental Security Insurance (SSI) for indigent patients deemed to be physically incapacitated. The wait for such assistance averages three to six months. The Division of AIDS Services arranges for supportive counseling, outpatient therapies, or long-term care services on an independent or group basis through public or private organizations operating anywhere in the municipality. Because it can take weeks or months to arrange for external services, counseling may begin in the hospital.

Canute sometimes feels that the doctors are rushing him out of the hospital. "They say that I have to leave because they need the bed; I'm told to go on welfare, they'll help me to find a place."

The processing of Canute's application for assistance

is unusually slow. Canute is eligible for SSI, but because of his dementia he must be discharged to a permanent residence providing 24-hour supervision. A long-term medical care facility is the only viable alternative for a patient with central nervous system toxoplasmosis, tuberculosis, anemia, seizure disorder, oral candidiasis, and herpes. Placement in such a facility involves processing numerous forms and interviews with the requisite case examiners and workers.

Patients who refuse to be tested for HIV usually do so out of fear, distrust of physicians, or impatience with the wait for results. Refusal to take the test results in an "HIV status unknown" designation in the medical record. The patient is not forced to take the test but will be treated for his or her current illness and then discharged. These patients are given information concerning HIV transmission and ways of reducing exposure to risk and encouraged to take the test at a later date.

If a patient refuses to undergo tests that could confirm an AIDS diagnosis, it is impossible to arrange for supportive services because there is no documentation of HIV status. These patients are treated for their current symptoms and then discharged. More often than not, they will return when they experience other, progressively worse, opportunistic infections.

Deborah is typical of such patients. She was admitted to the hospital four months earlier with the same symptoms and refused the treatment because it involved the insertion of a long tube down her throat into her lungs. After treatment with antibiotics her fever subsided, and within a week she was released. The caseworker encouraged her to stay with friends for a while and to take the HIV test, but there was no one with whom she could stay. She reverted to living on the street and in emergency shelters. Eventually she took the HIV test, which showed that she was HIV-positive. She had difficulty believing the results.

Now she is back in the hospital with accelerated

bilateral pneumonia complicated by alcohol liver disease, severe diarrhea, fever, and night sweats; tuberculosis has been ruled out. This is her fourth hospitalization in one year. She stays in the hospital only long enough to get her illness under control. When the antibiotic treatment produces some improvement, she leaves. Since she is not officially an AIDS patient, having refused testing, she will not be eligible for special public medical or social assistance. She will leave the hospital and resume life on the streets. Unlike the other patients who have been waiting in the corridor, she will not be taken to the AIDS ward.

3

The AIDS Ward

ONCE a patient has been admitted to a ward, the feelings of unfamiliarity begin to fade. Now the way the patient relates to the hospital procedures and staff depends on the patient's personality and past social experiences. Patients cope with anxiety in different ways. Some are simply resigned to the situation and accept whatever is said or done for them. Others, accustomed to indifference, are pleased when staff members attend to their needs. One patient, Santos, says, "At least in here I get a few things; food, caring people...a bed with fancy buttons, my own room. If I don't want to be bothered with anyone, I close my door."

Some patients seem to reach out to the staff. They are engaging, sometimes even charming. Some of this behavior is genuine, but for the most part it is self-serving and manipulative. Chatting with health care workers is often the prelude to a request for money or favors. Patients may initiate discussions with dietitians in order to obtain larger portions of food, or with nurses in an attempt to obtain higher doses of pain medication. One such patient, Brunilda, has a unique ability to draw one in with remarks like "Gee, you're cute, if only I were younger" or "Lighten up, it ain't the end of the world.... Don't worry, I won't bite you, but I can teach you a few things." She has a large inventory of dirty jokes that add spice to her conversation.

Canute is more pessimistic:

> Sometimes I think that the purpose of me coming
> into this world is to suffer. I've had a lot of bads
> and very few goods. My parents are very religious.
> They'd ask me to pray. For what? It never helped
> me. At least here I get help; warm, safe, I feel a
> little more secure. I'm surrounded by love and
> people that care about me. I got this fancy bed....
> When I scream, they come.

Anxiety causes other patients to retreat. They remain silent in their darkened rooms. Attempts to engage them in conversation are usually difficult and awkward. In Delores's case, for example, tests reveal the presence of HIV, tuberculosis, and PCP. Delores becomes
withdrawn and depressed for three days. She keeps the
curtains drawn and the lights turned off and refuses to
speak with anyone. Her appetite returns as her fever di-
minishes and her condition stabilizes. Gradually her sullen mood dissipates.

Lack of basic information about health care has dire
implications for the patient's ability to cope with illness.
Another problem is manifest in a historical lack of palliative care. Most of the patients in the AIDS ward have
not visited a health care provider in years. For example,
when Miguel is asked when he was last examined by a
doctor, he responds, "You must be kidding, it was back
when I was seventeen." This is Miguel's first hospitalization. He says he has never been sick and had no need
to see any doctors. He asked a family member to bring
him Nyquil (I watched him drink two bottles in 30 minutes), which he thinks will help, since "the doctors ain't
giving me nothing [for the pain]. I won't let them put
the intravenous in my neck. I won't let the nurse take
my blood...she's trying to collapse my veins."

Another patient, Remingo, shows me a scar under

his right arm. He has had stitches there for five months because he did not return to the clinic to have them removed. "Do you think they'll take them out here?" he asks. I encourage him to ask the doctors. "Ah, no me voy a molestar [I'm not going to bother]," he replies.

Patients frequently complain that physicians do not spend enough time with them, do not provide sufficient care, and do not explain diagnoses in terms that they can understand. Many complain about not being able to talk with their doctors—"I don't know what's wrong with me. They don't take the time to explain it to me!" Substance-addicted patients complain that physicians force them to undergo unassisted detoxification. Some claim that Methadone is not dispensed even when it has been prescribed, or that the amount dispensed is insufficient. Some of the intravenous-drug-using patients feel that the doctors want them to suffer. Often they ask me to convince the doctors to give them Methadone. The doctors' usual response is: "This isn't a detox center, let them wait!"

Under these conditions many patients feel abandoned, and this feeling is reflected in their comments. Says one, "Nobody came in to see me last night, I guess they gave me a break. I might be dead tomorrow evening, I need someone here to bear witness. I haven't seen my doctor in two days." Another adds, "They come in, I want to talk, but they ask how am I doing and then run out."

Discomfort and fear are heightened by the wait for treatment and information. After admission to a medical unit, patients become wholly dependent on the staff to meet their physical and emotional needs. Distrust and fear of the unknown permeate their experience. What they really want is attention and a chance to connect with the staff.

During a visit to Miguel I find the feeding tube disconnected. He says that it came out the previous afternoon. This observation prompts a discussion about the care he is receiving. "I'm a junkie, nobody cares," he complains. "I know how they are, they say, Oh! he's a junkie, let him suffer."

Yet within this environment there are some truly touching moments. Ambulatory patients can often be seen caring for others who are not able to care for themselves—feeding them, listening to their fears, cheering them up, and even negotiating their care. Sometimes patients coalesce into a group to support one another. They spend time talking about their respective diagnoses and ways of raising money for supplies (drugs, cigarettes, toothpaste, candy, etc.). Sometimes they panhandle in the hallways or lobby and recruit visitors to purchase things for them.

Networking among patients has some negative aspects. Gossip is a favorite pastime, but it can foster unnecessary concern and embarrassment. Of course, the staff officially refuses to share information about a patient with anyone except his or her relatives, but that does not prevent the patients from prying or from forming their own impressions. Generally, the gossip is petty in nature. It is unhealthy in the sense that the discussion revolves around superficial issues (body sores, hair loss) and obscures the real and debilitating issues affecting their lives: pain, mental incapacitation, poverty, fear, homelessness, substance addiction, helplessness, loneliness, and impending death.

Diagnosis and Denial

The patients' knowledge about AIDS is limited. They have a general impression that a "new killer disease" (also called "The Virus") is going around. The information is circulated by word of mouth. None of the patients can define HIV, although there is some notion of the means of infection or transmission. There is slight familiarity

with the diseases that can result and their progression. I
spend much time with them clarifying the issues of infection and transmission.

The dominant perception is that AIDS is a "gay
man's disease." Its recent spread among drug addicts is
sometimes attributed to an attempt to kill off heroin users: "The Man" [white power structure] is getting us
because we use *manteca* [heroin]." In this case ignorance is not bliss. AIDS is something to be avoided, but
how? As one patient comments,

> I don't think I got it from sharing needles. I don't
> share needles, I'm diabetic, so I get new ones all
> the time. Maybe I got it through sex with 'those'
> women. I really don't understand.

Other patients say that they "never felt that it would
happen to me. Before I really didn't care [about AIDS],
but now that I'm one of them, I think about it." Or, "I
haven't paid much attention to AIDS, even after learning [it was] the cause of my sister's death."

The AIDS diagnosis comes as a shock to such patients. Often they have no idea how they were exposed
to the HIV virus, and they spend a lot of time trying to
"make sense" of the diagnosis. David, for example, says,

> I know who I deal with and what I do. I wasn't
> thinking anything wild, like AIDS. This AIDS thing
> is far from my mind. You gotta give me good proof
> about this AIDS shit. I don't know what it is I
> got. I'm very careful with what I do and who I do
> it with....The body can't fight off that bacteria, it
> weakens their body so bad. I've seen people who
> had AIDS, they were very built and lost it. AIDS is
> a cancer, you can't stop it, regulate it, or control
> it. It will burn up your body.

I ask him, "Do you believe that you have AIDS?" "No,"

he replies, "no...I really don't know."
Another patient, Santos, says,

> AIDS...it's a bad disease, it's dangerous; they don't
> know much about it...people don't care...it's out
> of control. AIDS is underestimated; people don't
> see the importance of knowing about this killer
> disease. It drops your hair, gives you lesions. It
> gets your body. Sooner or later you're back to a
> kid. I've seen people drop like flies.

Esperanza's view of the disease is somewhat different. She belongs to a small subgroup of AIDS patients: those who do not smoke, drink, or use drugs. Her late husband was an intravenous drug user.

> You know what that means. I found out that Papo
> was HIV-positive in March 1988. The doctors
> wouldn't tell me what he had. On his death certificate it read cirrhosis of the liver.

She did not learn the truth until years later, when she herself was hospitalized with AIDS-related illness.
Delores blames the women's shelter for her illness. She first heard about AIDS in 1983.

> I didn't think that it would happen to me. I
> thought that the disease was basically a homosexual
> disease. I never thought that it would hit home
> the way that it has.

Even when patients understand the significance of the diagnosis, they have little appreciation of the fact that they must change their behaviors or that their past practices are linked to their current state. To reach this understanding, they need someone they can talk to about their feelings. They demonstrate a strong urge to engage the staff, friends, or family members in such conversations, but their family relationships are usually so fragmented that relatives resist these attempts. Thus, most patients focus on living as fully as possible while in the hospital and establishing contacts, if not bonds, with other patients or staff members.

Even when patients accept their HIV-positive or AIDS status, it is sometimes difficult to get them to connect this knowledge to the experience of the typical AIDS patient. They have difficulty believing that their situation will resemble that of individuals in other wards with more advanced forms of the disease. Moreover, established behavior patterns are not easily discontinued, especially when patients have been informed that they are suffering from a "killer disease."

Very few of the patients accept an HIV-positive test result or the diagnosis of an HIV-related illness without difficulty. Most fail to appreciate the long-term implications and focus instead on their present condition, which they decline to view as an AIDS-related illness.

Denial is also manifest in patients' refusal to associate specific behaviors with their impression of the "typical" AIDS patient. It is hard for any of them to see their past behavior as contributing to their current medical condition. They perceive their situation as unjust, even tragic. Ostensibly straight men with bisexual histories play down their homosexual activities. Heterosexual male intravenous drug abusers reject the diagnosis, citing the fact that they have never had sexual relations with men or shared needles with someone who "looks sick." Santos, for example, says,

> I left home when I was young. I started using dope—shooting cocaine for three or four years. I just fell into a crowd. I shared needles. I'm healthy...not weak, my hair ain't falling out. You can look at a person and tell [if they have AIDS]. Thank God I ain't caught no AIDS. The Lord ain't going to let me kick like that. I got luck, it stays

with me.

Larry's case is also typical. A 39-year-old black gay male, Larry entered the ER in a state of medical crisis. He was suffering from a very high fever, uncontrollable shaking, occasional memory loss, and blackouts. He was evaluated and then transferred to a medical ward. Tests revealed that he was suffering from cryptococcal meningitis. During his initial interviews with doctors, nurses, and social workers he denied practicing "at risk" behaviors associated with HIV infection. It was during subsequent conversations that he admitted to having had sex with multiple male partners. He regularly spent the nights cruising in his mother's car, "looking for trade."

Denial is often accompanied by withdrawal. Since many of these patients have had poor experiences with social service personnel in the past, they are distrustful and tend to ignore instructions or advice. They resist intimacy or sharing. Invitations to reveal their feelings to hospital social workers are rejected or else are accepted only after repeated explanations and encouragement.

Delores reacts in this way. Before her application for housing has been processed and the discharge planned, her fevers return. Another spinal tap is performed; it reveals that she is suffering from cryptococcal meningitis. The presence of another opportunistic infection terrifies her and she grows sullen. She is transferred to a semiprivate room and a few weeks later to a private room. "I want out of this place," she says. "It's getting me disgusted. They take out blood every two days, but the doctor doesn't explain. I'm just so disgusted."

Much of the denial and withdrawal exhibited by these patients is rooted in extremely low self-esteem. The patients have troubled lives, lives that in their own judgment have been disappointing. To them, a diagnosis of AIDS is par for the course. While AIDS was not expected, death certainly was. For some, death from a disease seems better than the kinds of death they face on the streets. These patients sincerely believe that their death will matter to no one. Miguel comments: "Me having AIDS...I'm a nobody. The rich having AIDS is a difference. They have money, I'm a nobody." And Santos adds:

> Where do you think they're going to put me when I die; in a 14-karat gold coffin? They'll put me in a bag and throw me in a ditch, [saying] he ain't nothing but a bum. I'm never going to get anywhere. I've always begged. I'm always going to be a bum.

Other patients adapt to the diagnosis of AIDS and the related illnesses by conforming to the hospital regulations and environment. At times they express anger or resistance, but generally they try to cooperate in order to obtain the care they need and speed the healing process. Their goal is to ease the pain, to survive and return to the life they know and understand. These are the hopeful ones.

Waiting to Die

Members of the middle class who contract AIDS usually have housing, financial support, health insurance, legal services, and access to psychological services. The medical treatment they receive is limited only by their ability to pay and their willingness to ask questions. This holistic approach to care may extend their lives. It can certainly optimize the quality of their lives for the duration of the illness.

Indigent patients have much less opportunity to request or obtain life-extending services. The disrepute and handicaps associated with their socioeconomic standing work against them to minimize the chance that they can live with AIDS in any meaningful way. They have little or no income, housing, family, friends, or insurance; they lack a history of health maintenance and experience in negotiating for services. For the most part they have barely survived, eking out an existence through marginal jobs, the underground economy, public assistance, or panhandling. They are downtrodden, alienated, and over-looked. When a highly stigmatized illness is viewed against this backdrop, the effect is inertia. They lose drive and passion. In their despair the spark of life fades. What is there to live for now: welfare, a single-room occupancy hotel (SRO), and care by people who presume that they are worthless?

Homeless patients often are so overwhelmed by their daily struggle for survival that any effort to cope with the implications of an HIV-related illness or HIV-positive diagnosis is postponed. Their focus is on main-taining an existence on the street, obtaining public assis-tance, finding space in a shelter or SRO, and getting money to buy drugs. As one patient puts it, "I don't even think about AIDS. There's so many other things...I can't remember one minute to the next." Hospital so-cial workers find that counseling sessions rarely go be-yond discussion of the patient's efforts to survive and to deal with external social service agencies. Esperanza, for example, tells me about a letter from her income main-tenance center informing her that her case will be closed because she did not attend the hearing. I attempt to calm her, offering to inform the center that she is in the hos-pital.

Some patients avoid conversations about their fears of illness and death. As Miguel comments, "I'm going to die and I'm so fucking scared...I can't talk about it, I can't handle the unknown." He mentions that during the past winter he bought drugs rather than coats for his children, but that "during the time I have left I'll try to leave something for my kids." Nevertheless, he has been giving money to visitors of other patients so that they can buy wine for him. Since entering the hospital he has drunk about a pint a day. Occasionally he asks them to buy heroin or cocaine.

Canute has lived on the streets since his teenage years. When he was first hospitalized for what now seems to be an HIV-related illness, the Human Resources Administration (HRA) placed him in an SRO. He feels lonely there: "I'm by myself and the home attendants won't come to the hotel." Whenever possible, he leaves the hotel, returning only when it is absolutely necessary. Now he's concerned that a lengthy hospitalization may have led the HRA caseworker to halt the rent payments, which would mean eviction.

Despite his discomfort and boredom, Canute is reluctant to leave the hospital because it would mean a return to drug dealing and living on the streets. "I don't want to leave the hospital," he says.

> When I'm alone, I know I will go back to doing drugs. I want to be in a place where people understand me. Nobody listens to me on the streets. I'm by myself. I ain't got nobody to turn to, my family don't care, they got their problems. What makes me go back to drugs is, if they don't care, why should I? I'm going to die sooner or later, what's my choice?

Michael is in some ways Canute's opposite. He is unemployed and has been homeless for two years, yet he is anxious to leave the hospital. "I was living in the fast lane," he says.

> I started using cocaine, then crack. I lost my job three years ago. My wife asked me to leave our home. After that I spent the winters sleeping on the trains, mainly because I couldn't stand the shelters.

He visited the soup kitchens and stayed with anyone who

offered him a place to stay. He has also had sex with "drug girls" while using crack. "As long as I am in this hospital I'll be depressed. I can't wait for the housing placement. I got to get out and start living again."

Among the patients on the AIDS ward are some who feel too beaten to struggle any longer. They know that there is little time left for them, so they simply wait. The waiting is sometimes tempered with anger, sometimes with stoicism, and sometimes with fear. Delores's crying fits increase in both frequency and intensity. She searches for some assurance that this is not "the end": "Why me? I was doing fine. I almost got out of this hell, I was feeling fine a few days ago." One evening it takes nearly continuous care and reassurance by caseworkers and nurses to calm her. We take turns holding and comforting her and encouraging her to maintain a positive attitude and get some rest in order to fight the meningitis. To her, this new infection represents "the plague." "This is it," she keeps saying; "there is no cure."

Over the next few days Delores tries her best to cope with her situation. Despite the persistent headaches, she responds to the new medication. The brown bag on the IV stand troubles her, as does the burning sensation in her veins, but she lies quietly resting in her darkened room, the shades drawn, the lights off, no visitors. Within three weeks she is dead.

4

Patients and Staff

THERE is no known cure for AIDS, nor is there a vaccine for HIV. Only the AIDS-related illnesses are treatable, and over time the virus weakens the immune system to the point where these illnesses do not respond to treatment. Thus, physicians have a number of options in determining treatment methods. Educated, middle-class patients are able to participate in these decisions, but the patients in Oremus Hospital typically are not.

Most of the patients have had no regular contact with a physician that did not involve a medical emergency. They have little experience with preventive or palliative medical care. Their modest education and meager medical experience preclude real understanding of the health issues they face, much less any informed basis for making decisions about their care.

Moreover, most of the patients arrive at the hospital in a state of physical crisis. Some are in advanced stages of AIDS-related illness. By the time they cope with the associated psychological problems, particularly denial, they have little emotional strength left for asking questions or making rational, objective decisions about medical care.

This situation serves to further complicate the patients' hospital experience. They have tremendous fear about being treated by strangers who now control their lives, apprehension about treatment processes they cannot understand, and anger about being "forced" into therapies, such as intubation and resuscitation, that seem to prolong their lives but also their suffering.

Individually, patients seek to maintain their separateness and make every effort to protect their privacy. They would prefer that no one be aware of their unconventional lifestyles or unorthodox behaviors. They will not reveal to other patients that they have AIDS until they are either forced or encouraged to participate in group sessions in which coping with AIDS is the topic of discussion. A few maintain this self-imposed exile because the other patients remind them of the people who probably exposed them to the virus. However, aloofness has its limits, which are usually reached at the onset of extreme illness.

The hospital prefers that patients remain isolated from each other. Communication and interaction put each patient at risk for opportunistic infections (especially airborne infections like tuberculosis). Some patients, however, object to the staff's efforts to separate them. Cory, for example, is angry at the staff and resents the infectious warning sign on the door to his room. He has ripped it down twice. "They have no right to advertise," he complains. Michael is also upset by the "precaution" sign on his room door. (All persons attempting to enter the room must report to the nurses' station.) He has removed the sign.

It is not unusual for newly admitted patients to remain distant from longer-term patients and staff members. They are often uncooperative and rebellious. But as the length of their stay extends beyond three months they begin to become part of the community.

The stigma associated with AIDS has an impact on every patient. Each arrives at the hospital with a history or an identity that is frowned upon if not condemned by the larger society. Society's negative view has been expressed so often and so definitively that the patients identify themselves as drug users, homeless, homosexuals, or prostitutes. The staff members respond accordingly and often treat the patients with disdain, even contempt. Among themselves, they speak of an individual's street activities or personal appearance in ways that serve to separate "good" patients from "bad" ones. They often express astonishment at the extent to which some patients are "caught up in their perverted activities." The patients are characterized as lazy, uneducated, dangerous thieves, faggots, and whores. The effect is discriminatory; "good" patients hospitalized with acceptable illnesses are treated more attentively and gently and with greater optimism than the "others." Michael complains that the doctors do not visit him anymore. "They make me feel dirty....I feel guilty being in this bed...I feel so ashamed." Another patient, Marlon, says, "I've done a lot of wrong things, I'm being punished....Something disastrous is going to happen. I will be destroyed, my body will be destroyed."

Hospital administrators are not concerned about the clash of values on the AIDS ward. The staff members are in control and are free to project their expectations onto the patients, who are powerless to do anything about it. So while staff members feel pity for patients suffering from terminal illnesses, they nevertheless limit their empathy or sympathy by blaming the victim: "They asked for it,...they did it to themselves,...they deserve it." One resident, new to the ward, exclaimed, "They're all AIDS here! If I knew I had AIDS like these people I would refuse treatment...I would kill myself."

Conformists and Misfits

In a broad sense, the patient community consists of two groups. The "conformists" have a vested interest in the smooth operation of the ward. They have come to realize that adequate care and supplies will not be readily provided unless they respect and adhere to hospital rules and procedures. This behavior is genuine, unlike that of the manipulative patients described earlier. These patients are likely to be outsiders in the general population, but within the hospital they seek to "fit in."

The conformists often intercede with the staff on behalf of patients who are experiencing difficulties. Likewise, they become a source of information for newer patients who are unfamiliar with hospital regulations, policies, and procedures.

Conformists scorn the second group, the "misfits." Few of the long-term patients fit this description, but many of the newer ones do. These are the ones who import and maintain unwelcome "street" behavior patterns. The conformists exercise direct pressure or invite official sanctions against certain actions of misfits, such as panhandling, robbery, and fighting.

Both groups include a subset of patients who may be described as "resourcers." These patients facilitate connections to the external world. They obtain drugs and cigarettes and share gifts and food with other patients whom they like. Canute points out that

> drugs come into the hospital by way of visitors and the staff. Sometimes the porter [sells] cocaine and heroin. He doesn't have to bring the works [syringe]...that's easy to get here.

Delores often receives visits from other patients and their friends. One of the latter is suspected of supplying drugs to a few patients on the floor. Delores's spirits improve after these visits. On one occasion I walked into her room to find another patient and two male guests present. Delores barely recognized me, and the other patient hurriedly left the room. One of the visitors wanted to know who I was and why I hadn't knocked before entering the room. The other slid a small brown bag down the front of his pants and left the room, commenting, "Damn, there's no privacy round here."

Regardless of the networking that occurs among patients, nothing eliminates the underlying fear that permeates their lives. Nearly all the patients retreat when faced with the physical reality of death. Few want to be in a room when a patient has a seizure or becomes violent with dementia. They do not want illness to disturb the tentative peace of the ward or the illusion of eventual recovery.

Delores is bothered by the candidness of certain other patients. She withdraws when one of them, Allen, says, "I won't be around forever, you better find someone else to grub cigs from." She is disturbed by the sight of other AIDS patients.

> I see myself. I get sick to my stomach. Whenever I think about AIDS I think of something dirty. I think of my past with drugs...and with men....I'm worried that I won't leave the hospital this time.

Miguel thinks he's getting weaker. It's difficult for him to see the other AIDS patients across the hall. "Being in the hospital is too much...so much sickness...I just can't handle what I'm seeing, [but] nobody talks about it. It's as if nothing is going on." Upon the death of another AIDS patient he remarks,

> I know I'm going to die. It's just a matter of time. I'm so alone. When I saw her swollen, sweating body...boy, she was bad. I'm just blank...just passing the day through. If I'm going to die, let it come.

Many of the patients deal with hospitalization in an uncooperative, demanding, angry manner. Some become nightmares for the staff, calling out to passersby or screaming at staff members, complaining about their food portions, their pillows and blankets, inoperative call buttons, and the like. Their requests are expressed impulsively and rudely, with no regard for—or perhaps even awareness of—the norms of social conduct. Esperanza is not impressed with her care:

> You see, you call a nurse [and] they say that the station is too far away to hear the calls. Sometimes the buzzer doesn't work, so I must yell for a nurse when I need one. If I could get out of the bed do you think that I would urinate in it? Damn nurses!

Esperanza's mother complains about her daughter's care on several occasions, and Esperanza has lodged a complaint with the hospital's Department of Patient Relations.

Another patient, Arturo, is harshly critical of the staff and the care he receives. He has recurring fevers and claims that the doctors have given him nothing for them. He threatens to leave the hospital:

> I might as well, sometimes there's only two nurses here working. They don't do nothing about my fever. My whole body aches. How the fuck can I be nice to the staff, when they don't do nothing for me?...My doctor is never here....Me encabrono [I get furious]. You got to get loud with the motherfuckin' staff. You ain't gonna play with me like a guinea pig. I yell at them. I'll get these motherfuckers.

Staff Reaction

Staff members react to these behavior patterns in various ways, depending on their own personalities, professional experience, and social background. They are frustrated by the fact that the patients do not appreciate how hard they have to work, their long hours, and the resource shortages they must contend with. Only empathy diffuses this frustration before it becomes anger or indifference. The "no fault" and gregarious patients are "adopted" and treated attentively. The withdrawn, sullen patients are reassured or left alone, depending on the demands of the day. In extreme cases, security guards are called to restrain or eject patients.

The nursing staff is most sympathetic to Esperanza. One nurse says that she is

> an innocent victim, not a drug user like the rest of them up here. Her husband was a drug user. I spoke with her, that girl never did drugs in her life. The doctors take a lot of interest in her case. They're attempting to arrest the meningitis and provide her with the necessary care.

Another patient, Milton, says,

> At least the nurses are nice to me....You know, they thought that I was a bum, I guess that's what I looked like when I came here. They changed. They treat me much better now....Some have given me reading material, candy, or just plain conversation. Others look at me as if I'm just a gay germ. They say, 'Are you, um...homosexual? What you been doing, boy, putting yourself in danger.'

The demanding or abusive patients cannot be completely ignored. Staff members attempt to be accommodating but at the same time remind patients that the staff controls their treatment and the length of their stay in the hospital. Reasonable wants and needs will be met according to an established schedule. There is a certain amount of resentment among staff members. Some of the nurses remark that the patients are better off in the hospital than they were on the street or in shelters. The implication is that the patients should be grateful for whatever care the hospital can provide.

Delores's case illustrates this point. Some of the nurses feel that she is much too demanding. "She wants this and that, wants me running with her medication, wants blankets, everything exactly when she wants it....She thinks this is a hotel." The nurses are put off by her screaming, panhandling of visitors, and "grubbing" of leftover food from other patients' trays. She often refuses to wear a mask (a protective measure used during the early stages of tuberculosis) and is often caught taking drags on other people's cigarettes.

Miguel is also viewed as uncooperative and demanding. He refuses to comply with instructions, especially regarding medication. He wants his bed changed every day and routinely asks for more than his share of snacks. "He thinks that this is a hotel....I've seen him on the street buying drugs. How is it that he doesn't get thrown out of here? He's done it [AIDS] to himself."

The difficulty here is that some staff members attempt to deal with patients as if they were fully competent and completely responsible for their actions. However, some of the patients are experiencing AIDS dementia, which affects the central nervous system and can cause incoherence, blindness, severe weight loss, weakness in the legs, listlessness, and loud, sometimes violent physical or verbal outbursts. Further complicating the situation is the fact that AIDS dementia "comes and goes." Such patients need extraordinary help to complete even the most routine tasks. Only a trained physician can recognize this ailment; the average nurse or nurse's aide at Oremus Hospital may not be sufficiently trained to recognize or respond appropriately to it.

Because of the limited knowledge and experience demonstrated by most patients, the medical staff assumes complete control of the treatment process. They see little reason or benefit in trying to educate patients at this "late" stage. It is unclear whether this attitude has a detrimental effect on the quality of care given or the sensitivity with which services are delivered. But I sometimes observe that patients, no matter how poorly informed, receive better, more extensive care when concerned family members or friends are regularly present at the hospital. These individuals are able to intervene as patient advocates, questioning the staff about medical services and negotiating better care.

Staff-patient communication is often strained. The physicians have a technical orientation. This is not to say that they are dispassionate, just that they attempt to be objective in their approach to medical cases. They are aware that most patients are unable to understand the intricate details of their condition. Their dialogues with patients tend to involve terse technical descriptions of illnesses and bodily functions. Nor do they spend much time with any one patient. Ordinarily there are too many patients and too few doctors to permit lengthy visits.

Depending the patient's mental state, it can be difficult to engage in thorough, well-rounded communication. Most people are apprehensive with AIDS patients. The level of apprehension may be heightened by the patients' perceptions of the hospital environment and the role of the staff. Terse, cursory, clinical dialogues with physicians can leave patients, especially non-native English speakers, feeling alienated and helpless. The result is often detachment from the staff as well as resistance to the prescribed treatment. Arguments, minor violence, and passive-aggressive behaviors are common.

The nature of the services provided to patients is strongly affected by the quality of staff-patient communications and relationships. Specific treatment and palliative methods are used in caring for these critically ill people. Yet when relationships are strained, incontinent patients may take revenge by defecating on the floor or pulling out catheters and IVs. Staffers respond by taking an inordinate amount of time to reconnect empty IVs or deliver medication. They concern themselves with rote tasks such as checking vital signs and keeping schedules current.

Lack of consideration can take many forms, some more subtle than others. Michael, for example, had planned to inform his wife that he had AIDS but had hesitated because of uncertainty about her reaction. Before he could tell her, an intern called her and advised her to undergo HIV testing. The wife inquired about the cause of Michael's condition, and the doctor felt that it would be unfair not to tell her the truth. This uncommon action left Michael irate. He threatened to sue the physician for violating his confidentiality and requested another doctor.

Little effort is made to communicate the reasons for certain practices and standards or to explain variations from normal procedures to patients or to their families and friends. Problems may arise when patients' feelings and perceptions are not considered in the provision of services or precautionary practices. For Canute, for example, being in the hospital, especially when restrained, reminds him of prison, a feeling that is intensified by the fact that he spent two years in jail for burglary. "You just can't walk out of here. It's like prison."

Allen also is restrained to his bed. "I am being persecuted," he complains. "They're going to keep me strapped in here. I'm not going for that shit. Why are you strapping me down?" In fact, the staff is afraid that in a disoriented state he might fall out of bed. He has exhibited somewhat violent tendencies in the past and has pulled out the catheter several times. He counters by saying, "If I'm going to die, let me die free. I don't want to be strapped down like some animal."

Esperanza adamantly refuses to submit to a fourth spinal tap. She believes that the previous taps are the reason she cannot walk. "If I'm going to die, let me die....I'm sick and tired of dealing with this."

Patient Resistance

Most patients resist the staff's ongoing requests for personal information, especially when the same data are reported to different people on numerous occasions. Their impatience is often translated into resistance to the routines of medical treatment—particularly the intravenous apparatus, blood pressure checks, and temperature monitoring. These treatment practices require cooperation by the patient, who seems to have no choice in the matter. When patients do not comply or participate in their treatment as expected by the staff, they are labeled "noncompliant." Their apparent resistance is noted in the medical record. This notation has implications for the manner in which successive caregivers relate to the patient. Chronic "resisters" or "troublemakers" tend to be avoided by the staff or are discharged at the earliest possible time with minimal assistance.

Resistance to treatment may represent an effort by patients to control some portion of their lives, to hold on to familiar patterns. The same may be said about resistance to recommendations that they modify certain behaviors, such as drug use. Thus, when Milton's pneumonia was brought under control he returned to the YMCA and visited the local outpatient clinic for follow-up treatment. At the clinic, he noted that accepting the diagnosis of AIDS was the hardest thing he had ever done. He is still "dibbing and dabbing with crack," claiming that it helps him "get it under control" or simply avoid thinking about illness and death.

Brunilda, who has had a drug habit for twenty years, says,

> I made my bed, now [I] sleep in it. You know you hear about this AIDS thing, but I just turned around and did it [shared needles]; having sex without condoms. That drug is powerful....I'm going to die using drugs.

She admits to bringing drugs into the hospital. About three months ago a friend in the hospital said, " *Yo te voy a curar*" [I will cure you]; she cooked up some *manteca* [heroin] and "hit" her. "Maybe it wasn't the right thing to do in the hospital, but when you're strung out or *enferma* [sick], only a true user knows the feeling."

Patients who resist or argue with the prescribed treatments in ways that are deemed antisocial or ignorant find their requests denied or ignored. At worst, an unacceptable manner widens the gap between health care worker and patient so that the quality of care is reduced. There are now fewer opportunities for patients to be educated, for understanding and acceptance to be enhanced. Ultimately patients are penalized for this behavior. I think the great demand for medical attention results in an overload of cases beyond the limit that can be served by the staff. In such a situation, they simply have no time to spare and little forbearance for the patient who creates "unnecessary" behavioral problems.

Fear of Contagion

Fear of contagion is a usually subtle, but sometimes obvious, impediment to treatment. Doctors, nurses, administrators, and others feel considerable trepidation in this regard. Their principal concern is being accidentally pricked by needles used to give injections to patients who are HIV-positive or whose HIV status is unknown. When such accidents occur, the hospital worker must undergo HIV testing every six months and follow CDC guidelines on needle sticks. Some are advised to take AZT for a year or until HIV status is confirmed. The following comments by a surgery resident are representative:

> I'm afraid, scared during surgery. Do you know how many needle "sticks" I've had? I've even had

an eyewash of HIV juice! I was doing surgery and it flew into my eye....Everybody should be tested. It's not right for me to face this risk. HIV testing should be pre-operation. Hey, I'd like to see my twenty-two-month-old son grow up.

A surgery intern had this to say:

Hey, we have a right to refuse treatment of a patient, especially if it's not for an acute medical distress—something life-threatening. If the person refuses HIV testing, why should I have to treat them? Why do I have to be put at risk? AIDS should at least be treated like other communicable diseases....There must be mandatory testing!

Cultural and Social Barriers

Cultural differences also affect relations between patients and staff members and the quality of care delivered. Most of the patients are of Hispanic, African-American, or Caribbean origin. Sometimes English is not their primary language. This is not the case for the caregivers, many of whom are of East Indian, Middle Eastern, African-American, or Hispanic origin, with varying degrees of English-language proficiency. Cultural biases, conflicting perceptions, and misunderstandings serve to postpone, delay, and hamper the quality of care given to patients.

Complicating the situation is the fact that a majority of the attending and resident physicians are foreign-born. They speak English with very heavy accents. Sometimes they do not understand what patients are saying, nor do the patients understand them. When both patient and doctor speak English as a second language, the barriers to communication are increased. And when a patient speaks no English it may be necessary to wait for hours or even days for a translator.

In their efforts simply to deliver medical care, the staff takes little interest in moving beyond cultural and language barriers. In response, patients withdraw a little more, knowing that they are not understood.

Within the hospital administration there is a faction that views AIDS patients as long since doomed to self-destruction by their dysfunctional behavior patterns. The fact that they are drug users, prostitutes, gay, illiterate, or homeless means, in the abstract, that there is little reason to go beyond basic care in addressing their medical conditions. There is an undercurrent of "blaming the victim," and it is manifest in the wording and tone of official documents as well as in staff-patient interactions. As Canute puts it,

> I don't hardly leave my room anymore. Most of my friends left or died. That's why you see me laying down. I feel sad. I say it this way, we all going to die. But let the man prove himself. We don't need to be treated like dogs. Some of the people [staff] in here ignore us. The doctors, nurses don't really care. At least they should let us die like human beings. They should listen to us once in awhile, that's all. That's all my friends wanted. You feel lonely in here, it's damn boring and depressing in here. I think it's important that people listen to us.

The fact that the patients are poor also implies that they are a drain on hospital resources. Without a doubt, when they are released there will be others to fill their beds. A certain amount of righteous indignation is expressed by staff members, especially residents. The lack of discipline and control on the part of some patients arouses their frustration and anger:

> We're wasting the taxpayers' money....We weren't
> trained to practice medicine under these condi-
> tions....How does society benefit from any of
> this?...They're disrespectful and very nasty . . . care-
> less and noncompliant...they don't deserve treat-
> ment. They're killing themselves....AIDS is God's
> punishment, look at the way they live, they have
> no values.

Staff members react negatively to patients' drug use
or addiction. Residents view with disdain and suspicion
requests for Methadone, even when the patient's par-
ticipation in a rehabilitation program can be documented.
Sometimes they acquiesce and prescribe the drug, but
on other occasions they deny such requests, forcing the
patient into "cold turkey" withdrawal. Similarly, health
care workers are impatient with intravenous drug-using
patients' pleas for pain medication. However, in their
weakened state these patients have unusually low pain
thresholds, so that average doses of opiates or
psychoactive medication may not succeed in relieving
pain.[1]
Staff members show little appreciation or understanding for the circumstances that produce antisocial,
self-destructive behavior on the part of patients. Conse-
quently, the patients are often left to cope with their disease and mortality by themselves. They are anguished,
and their cries just to be heard go unheeded. Again
Canute:

> They're all going to leave me, I can't blame no-
> body, when it's your time, it's your time...[but] I
> hope it's later, I don't want to die here. This [hos-
> pital] is a motherfucker, these people leave you in
> your room and shit, they don't pay attention to
> you. Yeah, they bring the medication and food,
> but that's it....After I die, I don't care what hap-
> pens.

The staff is under tremendous pressure to provide appropriate care. However, because of the overwhelming number of patients, the lack of adequate resources and personnel, and the hurried nature of the hospital routine, they become mechanical and even insensitive to the patients' needs. There are times, however, when residents, nurses, and other staffers display genuine altruism. One sees pregnant nurses tirelessly caring for patients with tuberculosis. Sometimes the staff brings in home-cooked meals for malnourished patients. Social workers bring them clothing and money to use for phone calls. Sometimes staff members just make the time to listen and to provide emotional support for patients struggling with their illness.

Application of Life-Prolonging Measures

There is little consistency in the application of modern technologies to prolong life. Some physicians hesitate to use those technologies on behalf of intravenous drug users and/or homeless AIDS patients who are expected to die soon. At times a "why bother" attitude was evident. At other times I would walk onto the medical ward and find that two or three people with AIDS were intubated (breathing assisted by a respirator). In these cases the physicians had chosen to aggressively prolong life in the face of a terminal illness. Some of these intubated patients bounced back; their lives were temporarily extended. Others died despite the effort.

In the course of my research I came to understand that the "do not resuscitate" (DNR) policy and the related use of cardiopulmonary resuscitation (CPR) are sensitive, complicated issues. Communication between patient and physician regarding DNR orders is limited. It seems difficult for the doctors to speak of life-prolonging measures with the patients, since most patients are in a state of denial or have some misunderstanding or misinterpretation of the diagnosis. Planning or preparing for death is not something they are ready to handle. Most often, the institution of a resuscitation policy is a decision left to the resident and/or attending physician.

The shortage of professional staff also affects the extent of life-prolonging measures exacted on behalf of AIDS patients. Sometimes there may be four or five respirators running in a twenty-eight-bed ward attended by two nurses and three aides. The extent of emergency care provided under such conditions is necessarily limited.

The staff may also have difficulty dealing with people who are struggling to live. As Elisabeth Kübler-Ross has observed, staff members "can do this only when [they] have faced [their] own fears of death...and become aware of...[their] own defenses which may interfere with...patient care." The development of such empathy or compassion would be a monumental achievement, for most staff members seem so overwhelmed by these terminal cases that they erect psychological barriers, thus stifling most chances for real introspection. Yet the staff is given little in-service training that addresses their need to cope with their own fears of death.

Perhaps more than any other social class of terminally ill people, these patients need professional assistance in coping with the inevitability of death. But there is no significant help for them. At Oremus Hospital the medical staff are overwhelmed by the sheer numbers of patients in their care, and the administration is burdened by state and local mandates and the cost of care. The medical staff needs to be trained and counseled so that the care they provide is the most empathetic possible and so that their own ability to cope is strengthened. Most of all, the staff must be held accountable for their responsibilities.

Notes

1. Barbara G. Faltz and Scott Madover, "Treatment of Substance Abuse in Patients with HIV Infection," in Larry Siegel, ed., *AIDS and Substance Abuse* (New York: Haworth Press, 1988).

5

Family and Friends

———

ARTURO has not paid much attention to AIDS, even after learning the cause of his sister's death. He has yet to tell his wife the truth about his illness. Perhaps she already has an inkling. "I'll tell her when I'm ready," he says. He is afraid that a hospital employee who resides in his wife's neighborhood will spread the word about his condition and perhaps tell his wife about it. I encourage him to break the news himself. "I don't think I have enough time," he objects. "I can't take the way life is treating me, maybe it's my fault. I'm just concerned that if my wife finds out, she just won't want me back."

The family plays a pivotal role in the healing process. The illness and hospitalization represent opportunities for the family to help the patient cope with complicated feelings about the disease and treatment. Solid, consistent, reliable, and trusted support from loving family members and friends can significantly affect the healing process. Such support constitutes a reservoir of strength and hope for the patient. There is no substitute for this emotional resource. No matter how attentive and caring the hospital staff and social workers may be, they cannot replace the nurturing provided by friends and family. This is evident in the case of Esperanza, who contracted AIDS from her intravenous drug-using husband;

he had not told her that he used drugs or that he shared needles with her brother, who later was diagnosed as having AIDS.

Esperanza is visited by her children and other family members. She is in good spirits. "You don't know how much I've prayed to God so that I can walk again....I want desperately to take care of my children again." Her mother prepares to do her daughter's nails and talks of frosting Esperanza's hair.

One day Esperanza's mother arrives with a home-cooked meal (arroz con pollo) and balloons. Esperanza is unable to go home for Thanksgiving, so the hospital gives her a food basket—turkey with all the trimmings. She hopes to be discharged before Christmas. Although she wants to leave the hospital, she's concerned about being unable to move about freely or care for her children.

The patients may have ties with parents, step-parents, siblings, step-brothers and step-sisters, spouses (both traditional and common law), "live-in" lovers and "special friends," extended-family members, friends, and neighbors. The intensity and quality of these relationships vary greatly. Some patients are close to their families and have well-established bonds with mates or "special friends." Even with the best of family relationships, however, patients feel bad about informing loved ones of their condition. They hesitate and postpone the revelation until they can feel comfortable speaking about it.

Many patients have strained relationships with their families. Often these are longstanding antagonisms. Great effort is required to overcome sour memories and infrequent contact in order to deal with the present medical emergency. Sometimes the "bad blood" cannot be overcome, no matter how much the patient might wish or need it. Typical is Deborah, who entered the hospital with a diagnosis of bilateral pneumonia. She was found lying unconscious in a parked car. She has a history of IV drug use and an alcohol addiction.

Deborah has been homeless for three years. She will not stay in the women's shelter because "you can get hurt in there." She has spent the past five years on the streets, sleeping in subways or sometimes with a "friend" who sells drugs, tries to make her "walk the streets," and beats her. She speaks of violence, prostitution, and drug use: "I was trapped. I was sometimes locked up in that house, he kept me drugged."

After she was admitted to the hospital her father and brother were contacted. At first the father did not want to have anything to do with her until she entered a drug rehabilitation clinic.

> All she ever was was trouble. After her mother died, all she wanted was to hang out with the wrong crowd. Don't ever call this house again! Tell her to clean her act up. After that she knows where I am if she wants to come home. Let her get welfare and into a program first.

She cries when I tell her what her father said. "He's a sick bastard. He's always given me a hard time. Doesn't he know that this time I have nowhere to go...and I'm really sick!" She continues angrily,

> That sick bastard tried to rape me, that's why I left the fuckin' house. I stabbed him in the stomach. It took twenty stitches to close that gut. I guess he can't forget that. Well, why would I want to go back there? All he's interested in is what I can give him.

Later I contact Deborah's brother, who resides with the father. After much persuasion he agrees to see her. Deborah is surprised when he visits. She cries and asks his forgiveness. She asks him to speak with their father. "All I need is a place to stay!" His only response is, "You know how he is."

The majority of the patients' relationships fall somewhere between the extremes represented by Esperanza and Deborah. Relatives sometimes demonstrate genuine care, sometimes total indifference, and now and then intimacy or estrangement. Attempts at reconciliation may be rebuffed, tenuously received, or fully accepted. The communication process is often an emotional roller coaster both for the patient and for the family, and sometimes the staff is affected. Consider the case of Milton, a thirty-two-year-old gay, homeless black male. His diagnosis includes meningitis, brain abscess, oral thrush, chronic wasting syndrome, and severe diarrhea. When we first met he had the covers pulled over his head, but in time he responded to me.

Milton obtained an associate's degree in 1978 and since then has worked at several odd jobs, most recently as a purchasing assistant for a local college. Nearly fifteen years ago he met and lived with a woman who later gave birth to a daughter who is now twelve years old. He has not seen the child or her mother for about five years. During a three-year period he maintained a relationship with a gay lover, who died one and a half years ago. The death and reduction in household income forced him to vacate their apartment.

Milton's sister and mother are aware of his sexual orientation, but he has not informed his father. The mother and sister do not accept his lifestyle. Their occasional visits to him in the hospital surprise Milton, since they will not permit him to move back home. "It hurts, but at least they pay for the TV," he comments.

At present Milton is staying with his grandmother, but she has asked him to make other arrangements. However, the illness has drained his meager resources. He has been technically homeless for the past year and has applied for SSI disability payments.

Milton is despondent about his family's rejection of him. He thinks about asking them for help again but is hesitant because of past rejections. Instead he asks another sister and an aunt if he can stay with them, but they decline, saying that they do not have enough space. "I'm very depressed," he says.

> I just want to forget all this AIDS stuff. I've been praying every day. I wish a miracle would happen. I'd like to start a new life, I don't want to worry about where I'm going after the hospital.

The last time Milton was hospitalized he attempted suicide; someone stopped him before he could jump out the window. He attributes the incident to despondency over his mother's attitude toward him. "I'm tired of being rejected by her, especially since I haven't seen my father since he left her."

Regardless of the closeness or distance between them, the relatives and patients are all affected by the stigma associated with AIDS. The extent to which they internalize this perception strongly influences their dealings with the patient, the staff, and the community.

One day Milton's mother brings him toiletries and slippers. Later he tells me,

> I talked with her. She says that she tries to understand this AIDS thing....doesn't want to change her lifestyle; she's not going to play nurse or disrupt my fifteen-year-old brother's privacy, since we'd have to share his bedroom. She said that the hospital will just have to find a place for me. She says I'll make it, like I did before. I can't believe how cold and insensitive that bitch is!

Gay Men

Gay patients have a particularly difficult time dealing with family and friends. The association of AIDS with homosexuality makes it difficult for them to divulge their medical condition to loved ones without revealing a closely guarded secret. Often they have led surreptitious, even duplicitous lives. They have grown accustomed to presenting one face to their family and another to a special public. The mask has been worn for so long that the prospect of its removal is frightening. Then, too, there is an awareness that the family may have known the truth all along. To destroy the illusion would shatter the uneasy silence and make everyone uncomfortable.

Larry has not told his mother that he has AIDS or about his sexual preference. He does not feel that she or other family members would understand his attraction to other men. Even in the hospital Larry becomes uncomfortable if we discuss this part of his life too openly. He is ashamed and scared and feels isolated. He is most concerned about his medical condition and its implications.

Societal condemnation of homosexual expression is sometimes intensified by unique cultural values and religious codes. This is particularly true for African-American, Hispanic, and Caribbean men. From time to time I encountered men who identified so fully with the proscription against homosexuality that they were unable to accept their sexual preference and usually developed close relationships with women in order to "prove" their masculinity. Of course, they did not disclose their bisexuality to those women. But once they contracted AIDS the secret could not be kept any longer, especially if they had no history of intravenous drug use.

Gay men without social support often mention that their friends or lovers have abandoned them. Only infrequently did I counsel patients who had long ago accepted their homosexuality and made it known to their families. These were the ones who had the healthiest relationships. However their families felt about their sexual orientation, it would not prevent them from providing support when it was most needed. Rubén is a case in point.

Rubén is a 24-year-old gay Hispanic male. After he was diagnosed with CMV, toxoplasmosis, and Kaposi's sarcoma, he told me that he had tested HIV-positive a year earlier. Rubén has a very good understanding of his diagnosis and prognosis. This is his second experience with toxoplasmosis (brain lesions), which causes dizziness and blurred vision. This hospitalization is difficult for him because the illnesses are becoming more severe.

I accepted it [having AIDS]," he says. "I know I'm going to die, that's it. I just want to have a good time now. I still like to go out and party with my friends, like go dancing and be with my ex-boyfriend. We were lovers for four years.

Rubén's mother is aware of her son's sexual orientation and the nature of his illness. She is very supportive and wants to take him home. She is, however, angry at the staff for not being attentive enough and for making him feel dirty because he is gay.

Look, my husband and three other children understand Rubén's lifestyle. We love him no matter what....All we want is to take him home. I know it will be hard, but we want him with us....Whatever time he has left, we want to be there for him.

More than any other subgroup of patients, openly gay men are likely to have the care and support of friends. Some staff members welcome the presence of those individuals, while others ridicule them and hamper their efforts to assist the patient.

Intravenous Drug Users

Patients who are intravenous drug users tend to have the most tenuous ties with family members. The criminal behavior often associated with drug use has created strains and breaches that cannot now be mended. Many of these patients have robbed or hurt their relatives. They have proven unreliable. These are the least trusted members of the family network and often have been estranged from their families for many years. In some cases the patient has no idea how to locate family members. Even when family members are accessible they provide only limited support.

A certain detachment is shown by family visitors. They perceive the patient's present condition as rooted in the same behavior patterns that caused so much pain in the past. They are unwilling to risk their safety and possessions to care for someone who has willingly chosen to jeopardize his or her life. Their visits are irregular and become less frequent over time.

Typical of these patients is Miguel, who is married and has two children: an eight-year-old son and a six-year-old daughter. Occasionally he lives with his wife, sometimes with other men, but recently he has been homeless. Miguel was sentenced to Almira State Prison for three years for armed robbery, and later to Rikers Island Prison for one year for violation of parole. While imprisoned he was homosexually active. Upon his release he met the woman to whom he is now married. He has never discussed his sexual past with his wife. "I'm not a fuckin' homosexual!" he insists.

> I was doing the fucking. Can't you understand I fucked those men, sometimes I stayed over their apartments, for money and sometimes for a place to stay. I stole from them to survive after my wife kicked me out.

Miguel's mother, wife, and sister visit him regularly. But often arguments break out and the visits are cut short. Miguel has told them that he has tuberculosis or pneumonia. They know about his *bicio* (habit) and attribute his deteriorated physical state to "the hard life he has lived."

Like some of their gay wardmates, some IVDU patients have succeeded in concealing their lifestyle from relatives. Disclosing that they are now suffering from AIDS-related illnesses would mean having to explain the probable source of infection. This dual revelation is a source of great stress and anxiety to these patients. Even more complicated are situations in which substance abuse is practiced by more than one family member. Fear of rejection is a major issue. Patients have difficulty accepting the medical diagnosis and are certain that family members will not be able to accept it either. Beyond this, they are afraid that family members will ignore their pleas for help, even when death is imminent. To avoid full disclosure of their condition, patients often tell their families that they have less threatening illnesses. Nevertheless, family members often became very concerned or suspicious, especially with repeat hospitalizations or when cases described as tuberculosis produce extreme weight loss or pneumocystis carinii pneumonia.

The family, too, may exhibit denial upon learning the true nature of the patient's illness. They cannot accept the fact that this could happen to one of their own. Such denial is complicated by unfamiliarity with AIDS and uncertainty about how the illness will progress. When family members are willing to permit discharge of the patient to be cared for at home, they often experience a sense of rejection and isolation from the community.

Marlon's wife assures him that she will take him home if he is discharged. She says she will do what she can. "I must do this," she comments. She agrees to take the HIV antibody test and, if she is infected, to seek medical treatment as an outpatient. The rest of the family will not be informed of the diagnosis; she is afraid of the possible reactions. Perhaps people will stop visiting her home or the city will take the children away.

Rubén's family signs him out of the hospital in order to take him home for a few days. When I telephone, Rubén refuses to speak to me. He is depressed and angry and does not want to speak with anyone. However, his mother needs someone to talk to and asks me to call again. She expresses a feeling that the family is totally isolated. "People [neighbors] just don't understand. ...sometimes I feel so ashamed." A gay men's support group has assigned a "buddy" to Rubén, but he does not seem to understand the family's cultural values and his caseload does not permit regular visits.

Sometimes a family's isolation is self-imposed. Relatives cannot bring themselves to discuss the situation with neighbors or even with extended-family members. When they do, friends fade away, contacts become less frequent, and dinner invitations are no longer extended or accepted. It is difficult to cope with the demands of at-home patient care. Community resources are too meager to make a significant impact on the lives of family members, which have become totally dominated by the emotional and physical care of a terminally ill relative.

Women and Children

None of the women patients were particularly concerned about AIDS before learning that they were HIV-positive. They express disbelief at the diagnosis of AIDS-related illnesses, which has been made after their hospitalization because of acute medical crises. They cite family responsibilities or lack of time as reasons for not seeking medical care at the first sign of illness.

For the most part, the women believe that they have been infected with HIV by their sex partners. None had any knowledge of their partner's sexual past or drug usage. They comment that they had great difficulty getting their partners to discuss their sexual history and that efforts to negotiate condom use were fruitless. They seem to have little control over their sexuality; their male partners are in complete control. Some of the women have been raped or have exchanged sex for drugs or money. A few speak of having been locked in "crack houses" for days or months, during which time they were forced to engage in sexual acts.

It is important to distinguish the intravenous drug-using women from those whose partners are or were IV drug users. Some of the women claim to have no experience with intravenous drugs or never to have engaged in sex outside of their unions, nor are they aware of such activities by their partners. They have fallen victim to their mates' behavior patterns. They are ill informed about the nature of drug use and similarly ignorant of AIDS.

The women who are in the hospital because of a history of intravenous drug use or prostitution exhibit the same strained family connections as the gay and intravenous drug-using men. They often report that their drug dependency began as a result of a relationship with a drug-using man. Once addicted, they frequently traded sex for drugs. Delores contracted AIDS in this way.

Delores has little education. After dropping out of high school she had a series of maintenance jobs, but it soon became clear to her that prostitution and drug dealing would bring in more money. The past eighteen years have been marked by drug abuse, prostitution, petty robbery, and homelessness. A month after entering the hospital she finally talks about her family. By her own estimation she has been a neglectful mother. She has four children between the ages of ten and eighteen. Two of them live with her sister; one, the oldest, is in Rikers Island Prison for attempted murder.

Delores's mother recently died of a heart attack. A sister died at the age of thirty-two of a massive stroke complicated by intravenous drug use. An intravenous drug-addicted brother, who frequently shared needles with her sister, died of AIDS-related illnesses during the same month. Delores also used to share needles with her sister. She has learned that her husband, who was absent for five years, recently died of AIDS-related illnesses.

The presence of children complicates the situation further. The children of these patients are most commonly in foster care or residing with relatives. The patients express love for their children and wish that they had been better parents. They hope to see the children again before dying, but often this is not possible.

The fear and confusion in the eyes of children visiting sick parents is heartbreaking. Such visits are likely to be limited. Often the caregiver is unwilling to bring the children to the hospital, feeling that the hospital environment and the sight of a suffering parent will be too difficult for the child to handle. Rarely are children adequately prepared for the death of a parent; in fact, they seem to be intentionally insulated from the prospect. When older children are informed that a parent has died of AIDS-related illnesses, they have little opportunity to discuss it with anyone. They are left alone and unable to deal with their grief.

Another tragedy manifest in these situations is the likelihood that the children have also been infected. Long after the mother's death, other family members, foster parents, or state agencies will have to deal with the painful maturation and slow death of these children.

The Homeless

The homeless patients have the fewest human resources to draw upon. They are the least likely to complain about the hospital facilities because they have the fewest options. There is no family to speak of; even if they know where family members are, the connection has been broken for so long that there is no chance of support now.

Remingo is typical of these patients. He is a thirty-six-year-old Hispanic male who entered the emergency room seriously underweight, with diarrhea and a high fever. He has a long history of intravenous drug use. He prefers heroin, but when it is unavailable he uses crack or cocaine.

Remingo is homeless and has lived on and off in various men's shelters. He would prefer not to return to the shelters after discharge because he has been robbed, mugged, and beaten by other shelter residents. He calls himself a drifter. When he does not stay in the shelters, he sleeps on trains or in abandoned buildings, sometimes with women who take him in when he has drugs to share. Eventually they kick him out. To survive, he steals car radios and food, or combs vacant buildings for scrap metal and empty cans. He explains: "When you got cash you got drugs, women, and friends."

His family lives in Puerto Rico, but he left five years ago because he did not want them to know he used heroin. Upon his arrival in New York he met a woman with whom he lived for a while. He and a friend started to deal heroin. After his girlfriend ran off with his partner, he started using more of the drug as a way of coping with the betrayal. Now there is no one in his life.

> You know it's been a while. I've gone from this one to that one. I just don't got no one to love me. I've never had that. I'm a loner, just surviving on those damn streets. It's hard in New York, people don't give you a chance.

Homeless women are the most vulnerable of these patients. They have led nomadic and violent lives. Many have witnessed the death of boyfriends, lovers, husbands, and friends as a result of AIDS.

Patients with Family Support

For patients with solid, supportive family ties, the picture is much brighter. Strong family ties not only improve the patient's ability to cope with the illness but also elicit more attentive responses from the staff. It's as if the knowledge that a concerned family exists inspires the caregivers to provide better treatment. Moreover, the closer the family ties, the more likely it is that the necessary lifestyle adjustments will be made in order to provide care to the patient. Even under the best of conditions, though, the road is a rocky one.

Consider Marlon. During a 23-day hospital stay he tried to come to terms with his diagnosis. He began to feel more comfortable with the fact that his girlfriend and family knew about his condition. They made preparations for his return home and pledged more honest communication. He promised not to use crack anymore. His main concern was what others might say if they found out that he had AIDS. He forbade anyone to tell his friends or the rest of the extended family.

Marlon's case was referred to the Human Resources Administration for SSI and supportive services. A few days after he was discharged I called him at home. His girlfriend said that he was very depressed and extremely concerned that people in the neighborhood would find out about his diagnosis. She found the HIV testing process very stressful. Even though she had tested negative, she felt that she was not out of danger and planned to be tested again in six months.

The situation took its toll on their relationship. "I'm just the housemaid," she complained.

> He doesn't want to marry me now. I'm not going to leave him, I'm forty-six years old. Do you think it will be easy to find someone else now that I may be infected?

A week later I spoke with Marlon. "I haven't been keeping my appointments with the outpatient clinic and slipped back to doing a little crack," he told me. His relationship with his girlfriend was strained and he was not sure what was going to happen. He agreed to visit with me at the hospital, but never showed up.

Family dynamics have a significant impact on the prospects of terminally ill patients. The patient struggles against physical deterioration and emotional turmoil. Depression, confusion, and hopelessness affect the will to heal and, hence, can make the difference between tentative recovery and rapid decline; between cooperation with the treatment and helpless acquiescence to sickness.

Family and friends are a source of comfort both in the hospital and, in some cases, during subsequent home stays. The extent to which they provide emotional support seems to affect the degree of well-being the patient experiences. Unconditional love and genuine bonding are welcome ingredients in the patient's mix of daily experiences. However, family members who provide support, but with their own agenda, may create additional strain. Some family members may become interested in the financial benefits received by the patient, using them to supplement their own income. Others want to take control of the patient, insisting, for example, that the patient join a particular religious organization.

Patients who are viewed as "innocent victims" are given the most support by their families. Family members react with sympathy and compassion. Support is readily available in the form of regular visits, gifts and flowers, food, babysitting, and the like. These "innocent victims" contracted AIDS from partners who, without the patient's knowledge, engaged in risky activities such as intravenous drug use, bisexuality, or unprotected heterosexual sex.

Regardless of the nature of family support, there is one issue that patients must face on their own: their impending death. Thoughts of self-punishment, second chances, and religious deliverance pervade their consciousness. I am troubled by the sheer weight of the pain and loneliness these patients feel. As Michael puts it,

> I think about dying a lot. I think about the kids. I think about the things people say if you're a junkie....they think you don't care about your kids or your family. I'm scared of dying. I won't be able to take it. I'm scared of being alone....If my wife gets the disease, I will fuckin' kill myself....What will I do, who will take care of my kids?

6
Death and Dying

"W HEN is my day going to come?" Esperanza wonders. "I don't know when I'm gonna die. It's funny, you know when you're gonna be born, but you don't know when you're gonna die."

As much as the word is used in everyday conversation, we do not know much about death. Emily Dickinson called dying "a wild night and a new road." The unknown and implacable nature of death colors the experiences of patients and staff alike on the AIDS ward.

For AIDS patients, death is a much too personal thing to treat abstractly. They expected death to be like walking through a minefield: instantaneous, without warning or time to react. They did not expect to die by degrees. For the person with AIDS, death occurs in protracted stages, by inches; through doctors' visits, restrictive diets, medical crises, a multiplicity of medications, weeks or months in a hospital, and then the worst: heart seizure, cancer-ridden organs, or respiratory failure. Much of this process unfolds during a stay of several weeks or months in a hospital.

With hospitalization comes time to think. The patients dwell on the factors that contributed to their maladies (substance abuse, risky sexual practices, inadequate health care, joblessness, homelessness). They reflect on their lives, on the decisions and choices they have made. In time they begin talking about their experiences, disappointments, achievements and failures, triumphs and regrets. For those with intact familial or other social ties, there is concern about how to "tie up loose ends" and bring closure to their lives. Zita, for example, must make plans for her children. "This is something I never expected. [It has] really knocked me off my feet." She wants me to contact a lawyer who can finalize her plans for having the children adopted. Yet she also speaks of wanting to leave the hospital in order to start a new life.

Many of the patients progress through the five stages of dying described by Elisabeth Kübler-Ross in *On Death and Dying*.[1] The first stage, denial, presents a formidable challenge. According to Kübler-Ross,

> Denial functions as a buffer after unexpected shocking news, allows the patient to collect himself and, with time, mobilize other, less radical defenses. ...This anxious denial following the presentation of a diagnosis is more typical of the patient who is informed prematurely or abruptly by someone who does not know the patient well...without taking the patient's readiness into consideration.[2]

Denial is usually a temporary defense; it is soon replaced by partial acceptance. In this stage patients seem to be observing their own demise, going along with the program and procedures, the doctor's judgment, and what they perceive as their fate. They feel powerless to affect the quality or amount of care they receive because they believe that it will not change the outcome. At the same time, most manage to convince themselves that they will recover, partly because they know so little about AIDS-related illnesses and partly because they have survived so many other trials. They want and expect to leave the hospital.

Denial is understandable when it is viewed against the pattern of the patients' lives. Many AIDS patients have behavioral histories rooted in denial. Sheppard Kominars makes this point in reference to gay men and women:

> We have been conditioned...everywhere in society to be victims and to deny what is, and to accept what is not. Under these circumstances, it is little wonder that gay men...are at such a high risk for addiction...a disease of denial. Becoming addicted was the only way to stay sane....[This] made it possible to put up with the cruelty and abuse, the hatred and discrimination, the distortions of truth that...gay men experience.[3]

A few of the patients remain in the denial stage throughout their hospitalization. Most, however, maintain a partial denial throughout the dying process. These are the ones who cannot develop other defense or coping mechanisms. As Kübler-Ross explains,

> The need for denial exists in every patient at times, at the very beginning of a serious illness more so than towards the end of life....Depending very much on how a patient is told, how much time he has to gradually acknowledge the inevitable happening, and how he has been prepared throughout life to cope with successful situations, he will gradually drop his denial and use less radical defense mechanisms.[4]

Canute's case illustrates this process. Canute believed his illness to be a *maldicion* (evil spell). "I can't do nothing," he says:

> work, sex, *no se me para* [my penis doesn't get hard anymore], I don't have no feelings. I can't do what

> I used to do.... Everybody has to go sometime. At
> least nobody killed me, nobody hurt me.

But he admits that he is afraid.

> You never know when it's going to strike, you
> know, sickness and death....They're all going to
> leave me, I can't blame nobody, when it's your time,
> it's your time! [But] I hope it's later.

> I don't want to suffer. I ask God to take me, take
> me, let me know when. I don't want to suffer. I'm
> not scared. I'm tired of suffering...just get it over
> with. If I could find a way I would do it myself.
> I'm tired of this, wasting my time, wasting the
> doctor's time. I'm tired of all this shit.

Other patients talk about the futility of medical
treatment. In their denial, many focus on the opportunistic infections for which they are being treated, or on
another disease that is deemed socially acceptable. They
convince themselves that they have something other than
AIDS, such as pneumonia, bronchitis, or cancer. Generally, they refuse to believe that they have AIDS and work
to convince themselves and others that they have a temporary infection or a curable disease.

The second stage of the dying process outlined by
Kübler-Ross is anger:

> When the first stage cannot be maintained any
> longer, it is replaced by feelings of anger, rage, envy,
> and resentment....This stage is very difficult to cope
> with from the point of view of family and staff.
> The reason for this is in the fact that [anger] is
> displaced in all directions and projected onto the
> environment, at times almost at random.[5]

Among patients on the AIDS ward, disappointment or dissatisfaction may be represented in negative behaviors. They may begin to refuse treatment or start fights with staff members or other patients. At the root of these behaviors is fear of abandonment. The patient lashes out with anger because his or her spouse or parents, or society in general, have failed as a benevolent source of nurturance.

The experience of anger is tied to the stigma of AIDS. Before the diagnosis, the patients had a preconceived notion about the "kinds" of people who are most likely to contract AIDS. Although they have limited knowledge about the transmission and progression of the disease, they view AIDS as a plague and people with AIDS as pariahs to be despised, feared, and rejected. This prejudice, together with stereotypes about poverty, addiction, homelessness, homosexuality, or prostitution, prevents them from accepting the fact that they have been diagnosed as suffering from AIDS. The perceived, sometimes actual, indifference, insensitivity, or contempt of staff members reinforces negative stereotypes and further isolates the patients from each other while undermining their ability to accept their own mortality.

If a patient is unable to cope with denial and anger, he or she enters what Kübler-Ross defines as the bargaining stage—"an attempt to postpone." This stage

> includes a prize...for good behavior, [often assuming] a deadline, and...includes an implicit promise [not to] ask for more if this postponement is granted...Psychologically, promises may be associated with quiet guilt....The patient needs trained facilitators who can help resolve irrational fears or the excessive need for punishment.[6]

Delores's case provides an example. She consistently denies the veracity of her diagnosis. Each time we talk about her condition she concentrates on a particular illness, such as tuberculosis. She is angry about her experience with drugs. She eventually enters the negotiation stage, talking about her family and wishing that she could be different with them. She tries to convince the staff that she can care for herself: "I can live on my own, I won't take any more drugs or have unsafe sex." At the same time, she asserts a seemingly contradictory drive to survive:

> I'm going to kick down to the last [breath], with God's help maybe I'll be here for ten years....When I get out of here I want my own room. I don't want to be with anyone. Shit, I refuse to go down. I want another chance.

When terminally ill patients can no longer deny the nature of their illness and the certainty of death, they are consumed by dread. Anger, rage, stoicism, carelessness, or indifference all fade in the face of a sense of great loss. This is the fourth stage, depression. According to Kübler-Ross, this depression may take two forms.

> One is a reactive depression...the person has no difficulty eliciting the cause....The second type is a preparatory depression...rooted in sadness about impending losses.

In the depression stage most patients react to the diagnosis as if it were a death sentence. With the shock comes emotional and physical withdrawal. They are less communicative and keep to themselves in darkened rooms, lying listlessly in their beds. Withdrawal turns into anger, then depression, both of which are rooted in nonbelief.

In time there is a tentative recovery from the emotional distress. If they are able to do so, patients sit up in bed or venture out into the hallways. They engage other patients in conversation, finding similarly diagnosed individuals with whom they can discuss their medical situation and commiserate. Occasionally they invite these newfound friends into their rooms. Other patients never achieve this transitory emotional recovery. They internalize the diagnosis, remarking that there is nothing they can do about it except wait for what will happen next. A few believe that they deserve such an end. As their medical condition deteriorates, they become weaker and revert to hiding in their rooms. It becomes clearer that death is near. Their new friends, who may not yet be experiencing similar symptoms, are put off by the sight of their decline and visit them less and less frequently, then not at all. Most of the healthier patients find it too difficult to watch their physical deterioration. Some express disbelief or repulsion and hope that the same thing will not happen to them. Others are curious, but they still do not want to see or know too much. Perhaps by turning away from the reality of death they can postpone it or avoid it altogether.

One of Canute's friends died in the hospital. "That hurt me," he says. "I used to [come here to] feed him...tell him that he was not going to die....I think it's bad...I don't want to get to that moment...you know, die."

Another patient, Anne, has become increasingly traumatized as her disease has progressed. On two occasions she has passed out. This is frightening and increases her feelings of depression. She begins to withdraw. I find her lying in bed in the fetal position. She prefers to leave the lights turned off and the door closed—"I want to be alone." When she speaks to me she appears confused, unfocused, and disoriented. "What's gonna be is gonna be. I'm gonna die, [but] I just can't think about it." Beyond this, Anne will say nothing of her feelings about death and dying.

Patients often think about suicide. Do they wish to choose the time of their death and avoid the waiting and suffering, or is suicide the ultimate act of despair and hopelessness? Canute says, "Sometime, I think of 'cutting up,' you know, like cutting myself or some stupid shit." During previous discharges he has attempted suicide by way of overdose. He was readmitted when opportunistic infections left him unable to care for himself.

> Don't get me wrong, I have had ideas. But I don't
> care no more. I don't want to live. I've lived my
> life. I'm exhausted. I'm bored, disgusted. I feel
> like giving up.

These remarks prompt me to refer the case to an in-house psychiatrist. Upon consultation with the attending physician, the psychiatrist prescribes Cojenten and Haldol.

The last milepost on the approach to death is acceptance. According to Kübler-Ross, if patients are to die in a state of acceptance and peace they must have been able to work through their anguish and anxieties. Only with the passage of time do patients reach this stage. When they do, they are no longer depressed or angry about their "fate." They can now

> express...previous feelings...envy for the living and
> the healthy...anger at those who do not have to
> face their end so soon [and] contemplate the coming end with a certain quiet expectation.[7]

The patients who reach the acceptance stage are likely to have above-average social skills, intact family relationships, and, often, religious beliefs. They achieve a level of freedom that seems to be rooted in profound trust. These are the ones who are victorious over disease and death. They have found the courage to be who they really are, without apology.

When Alberto is finally able to accept his impending death he becomes uncustomarily frank and open. "I know what I got...*la Sida* [AIDS]," he says. "I got my days...I'm going to try and take care of myself. How long do I have to live?" He knows that he will not recover and copes by remaining very still in his room, alone and in prayer. There is a calm, quiet strength about him. He walks the corridors carrying the Bible his mother left for him, proudly wearing a new set of rosary beads around his neck.

The most usual vehicle for achieving acceptance is a turn or return to religion. Faith does not wash away the tears, but it does help the patient live with integrity, trust, and hope. Death, when faced directly, apparently can be a great liberation. Part of dying is letting go, throwing down the burden. Patients who face death are freed from injustices and betrayals, from the sickening smell of their own wasted bodies, and from their own cowardice.

Jerome spends a lot of time talking about his faith in God. Sometimes he asks me to read to him from the Bible. He likes to listen to religious music, so I secure tapes from his church and borrow a tape player from the hospital. Jerome says little about death ("[That's] in God's hands"); instead, he dwells on recollections of what life has been like for him. In his frame of reference, his life is over.

When a patient is near death and the staff has decided not to artificially prolong life, there are visible cues that are observed by the other patients. The sight of patients dying unattended is traumatic for the others because their situations are so similar.

When Canute enters what will later be called the "final stages," he floats in and out of consciousness. There is no one to cut his hair, and his beard has grown long and unmanageable. His face is distorted by pain; one eye is nearly closed. He cries incessantly and often yells for help. He has to be restrained.

Over the next few days he grows weaker. In a barely audible voice, he complains about the pain. It is difficult to watch his slow descent into death. We sit quietly together for awhile, then he asks, "What do you think is happening?" As I respond, he closes his eyes as if he does not really want to know.

The obvious physical decline and pain are not enough to make him confront death. His fear of death prevents him from talking with me about his feelings.

The routine of the hospital goes on all around him, seemingly oblivious to his dying. During the last few days I stop by his darkened, silent room to find him lying in the unlaundered sheets, staring blankly at the ceiling, his face unshaven, hair uncombed, and meal trays untouched.

Alone and in pain, dying patients are at the most vulnerable and helpless point of their lives. Their fear and hurt are difficult to express, especially since there were so few people who listened to them before they became ill. Their isolation is intensified by the fact that most of them have strained family ties—if they have any at all. Their relatives had little reason to contact them when they were in good health and have little incentive to be supportive as they die. The homeless patients have few friends in the community who could offer support and usually die alone. Canute, for example, declined to be visited by the hospital chaplain because he feels that it is "not time yet." There is no one to hear his struggle. He is left alone except at meal and medication times.

Waiting to die is difficult, especially when there are so few opportunities for distraction. Escape from the hospital is a familiar theme. Most of the patients want to live the way they have been accustomed to until "their time comes." The medical ward is often viewed as a prison death row. Patients express feelings resembling those of a convict who has exhausted the last appeal. Reprieve has been denied; they must endure the pain and discomfort until it is time to die.

Anne's remarks are typical. "What's happening? I know I'm going to get sicker....I'm a fighter, I'm a Cancer. I leave it in God's hands. If it ain't my time, I'm not going nowhere."

Days later Anne remains on the respirator. The doctors expect renal failure. We spend time together quietly. When I hold her hand her eyes open and she winks at me. She struggles to breathe, even on the respirator. She is terribly afraid, and I tell her it's okay to let go if she wishes. I wipe the tears from her eyes. She winks again and clasps my hand. Moments later she is dead.

The Protocol of Death

At the demise of a patient the staff assumes a purely utilitarian function. When the physician pronounces a patient dead, a team of nurses' aides (two or more) prepare themselves outside the room, donning masks, gowns, and latex gloves. I have been granted permission to observe the process, so I don similar protective garb.

The room is just as I had left it. The machinery is still there and the room is in disarray. There is dried blood on the floor. The motionless body rests on its back, the bloodstained gauze pads scattered about the bed where they fell when the patient last struggled to breathe.

First the life-support machines, if any, are disconnected. It is important to avoid any body fluids that might ooze from points where catheters or other tubes have been inserted. Such tubes and other disposable machine parts are discarded in a red plastic bag (the color indicates that the bag contains hazardous infectious waste).

One of the nurses removes the IV tube from the patient's upper arm, then the ING tube from his nose. She pulls back the top sheet and removes the catheter from his penis, saying "Hey, you got to be careful with how you remove these tubes...this stuff is dangerous." The tubes are disposed of in the specially marked bags.

Together we push the body forward so that one of us can remove the sheet from beneath him. Next, the hands are crossed, secured with surgical tape, and placed on the chest. The ankles are similarly secured.

The team is careful to guide me in the handling of the body. "Just do it this way, we won't have no seepage. We got to be careful with body fluids....Just do as I tell you."

We roll the body to the right-hand corner of the bed and roll a new sheet under the midsection. A similar move is carried out to the left in order to spread the sheet completely under the corpse. A mortuary tag is tied to a toe and, beginning at the head, the torso is wrapped in gauze. Next, the body is neatly wrapped in the sheet. All is ready for the staff member who will take the body to the morgue.

A Lonely Death

The isolation of the AIDS patient continues even after death. Often unclaimed bodies remain in the hospital morgue for days or weeks until relatives are found and come to claim them. Others are simply interred in municipal paupers' graves. In Canute's case no one comes to claim the body. Attempts to contact the family are unsuccessful. The body lies in the morgue for some time. Eventually Canute is buried in Potter's Field.

A strange silence surrounds the death of an indigent AIDS patient. The time between diagnosis and death is so short that friends and family members have little time to cope with their disappointment, sorrow, or anger, let alone the economic, social, and psychological problems attending the illness and eventual demise of the patient. They often express a sense of helplessness. In many instances this feeling is not new; they have felt it in failing to help the deceased cope with drug or alcohol dependency, joblessness, or perceived sexual deviance. A few stay away as "the end" approaches in order to avoid facing their emotions and the reality of death.

In cases in which the family was close to the patient during illness, hospitalization, and death, there are strong expressions of grief and guilt. Many family members and friends express concern that they or other family members will suffer the same fate because of possible exposure to the illness. It is not uncommon to hear that other family members or friends died of AIDS-related illnesses. Now their grief and worry is compounded.

It also is not uncommon for the dead patient's family or friends to express anger. They are angry because the deceased "brought this on the family or exposed me to this." "It's been hard dealing with the fact that he's a homosexual [or drug addict], but now we have to deal with this AIDS thing!" Many feel embarrassed and humiliated. They express the wish that "the whole thing be over." While they wait for "it to be over" there is silence and isolation.

Surviving children are probably least equipped to cope with their parent's death. If possible, they will go to live with other relatives, usually grandparents. There is no way to forecast the long-term implications of the patient's death for those relatives.

Death does not discriminate according to economic status. But upper-class Americans, even those dying of AIDS-related illnesses, go through the process with varying degrees of assistance and support from health care professionals, medical and psychological resources, family, friends, and the broader community. Even with the knowledge that death is near they continue to deal with life and living, even if in a restricted manner. They have the opportunity to resolve old conflicts, "tie up loose ends," and make the necessary preparations for those who will survive them. After their death the community comes together in a public way to bid farewell, eulogize them, and remember their contributions.

Poor and solitary patients with AIDS must deal with death and dying in isolation and ignorance. They are totally dependent on the care and good will of social institutions—hospitals, public assistance organizations, and the like. But there can be no human bonding here. I have watched these patients die in silence and alone. The last human beings on earth to be with them, the hospital workers, are emotionally detached from them. There is little touching, comforting, or even grooming. Few staff members have the inclination or time to help patients cope with the approach of death. With no one to talk to, their fears go unchecked, the "loose ends" are left untied. There is no concern about Last Wills and Testaments. What do they have to leave anyone? There is no one to give them hope, no one to make them feel brave or worthy. After they die, they are unceremoniously discarded, as they were in life.

Notes

1. Elisabeth Kübler-Ross, *On Death and Dying* (New York: Macmillan, 1969).

2. *Ibid.*, p. 39.

3. Sheppard Kominars, *Accepting Ourselves* (San Francisco: Harper, 1989).

4. Kübler-Ross, *op. cit.*, p. 42.

5. *Ibid.*, p. 50.

6. *Ibid.*, p. 83

7. *Ibid.*, p. 86.

8. *Ibid.*, p. 112.

7

Issues and Implications

NO hospital is typical. Just as no nation or community or family can represent all others, neither can the experiences of indigent AIDS patients and staff at Oremus Hospital be generalized to all other hospitals with AIDS wards populated by poor and extremely troubled patients. But on the basis of many conversations with AIDS caregivers at other hospitals in my own and other cities, it is safe to say that neither are the situations in this book unusual. Among the many policy issues raised by the experience of patients and staff at Oremus Hospital, perhaps the most universal are those involving confidentiality, the treatment of intravenous drug users, the need for greater options in palliative care and supportive services, and the larger issues of health care for the urban poor, which are highlighted in the extreme by indigent AIDS patients.

Issues of Confidentiality

The American medical profession has a long tradition of respect for the rights of informed consent, confidentiality, and privacy. The potential risk to patients of unilateral disclosure of their AIDS status is real and significant. The public's widespread and general lack of sympathy, sometimes even hostility, toward infected individuals is well known.

Nevertheless, the issue of confidentiality is a potentially explosive one. Early in my study, the room doors of patients who were suspected of being HIV-positive or of having AIDS displayed red signs instructing visitors to stop at the nurses' station before entering the room. Later this practice was halted because of complaints by patients and relatives, but the use of red trash container liners in those rooms continued. For those who recognized that red liners are used for the disposal of hazardous infectious waste, the liners served to advertise the patient's HIV status.

Similarly, the staff is placed in the awkward position of withholding information about HIV or AIDS status from friends and family members if the patient so desires. Some patients willingly inform others of their diagnosis, but in most cases this happens only after several counseling sessions. However, there are many cases in which wives, lovers, or pregnant girlfriends cannot be told the truth about a patient's status because of the latter's refusal to reveal it. Fear of rejection, embarrassment, or simple irresponsibility prevent the patient from sharing this information with those who have a right to know. In potentially life-threatening situations moral suasion is applied. But in too many instances the news is revealed after the patient's demise, leaving the medical, nursing, and social service staff to cope with the outrage of family and friends.

Special Issues in the Care of IVDU Patients

Drug use is such a prominent feature in the lives of these patients that it deserves special attention. Many drug-addicted patients indicate that they understand how HIV is transmitted. However, most feel that their drug habit is so profound and extends over so long a period that, despite their awareness of the risks, they consciously choose to continue using drugs. They rationalize their behavior by saying that it is hard to enter drug treatment programs because of the shortage of treatment slots and the resulting wait for admission. Many said that they prefer using drugs over facing the reality and implications of AIDS. Others say that the people with whom they were sharing needles "looked clean," meaning that they did not believe those individuals were infected.

As the AIDS epidemic has unfolded, cases involving intravenous drug use have increased dramatically. Although knowledge that HIV can be transmitted via shared needles or "works" has circulated among the drug-using population, few of the patients believed that they would be infected. A sizable percentage of the patients make comments such as "Yes, I shoot drugs, but I have my own works and I never share with anyone" or "I know who I share with, and they don't look like they have AIDS."

Some IVDU patients seem resigned to their illness: "Hey, you have to pay the price....I've spent so many years chasing drugs that I just can't stop....It's a way of life for me...AIDS is the consequence." Perhaps this reaction is a reflection of the acquiescence with which they have accepted so many other disappointments in life.

It is not surprising that some of the patients continue to use drugs. Among substance abusers, denial is a defense against dealing with the consequences of addiction. However, I observed resistance to stopping drug use even among patients who accepted the fact of their AIDS diagnosis. "I've been doing this all my life, I'm just not ready to stop now." Others see hospitalization not only as a way to obtain treatment for AIDS-related illnesses but also as an occasion to seek help for their drug addiction. Scarcely available drug rehabilitation programs and the lack of suitable housing undermine this effort, however. Then, too, patients with prior experience with rehabilitation programs perceive them as having limited value: "They take you off one drug and put you on another one [Methadone]." They also do not feel comfortable with the overcrowding and restrictive rules of rehabilitation clinics.

Those expressing such views say that they want to manage their own addiction through continued, albeit "safer," use. They believe that getting off drugs would have a minimal effect on their lives. They would still have marginal job skills and fragmented links to the community. "What will I do with myself when I'm clean [drug free]?"

Within the hospital, substance abuse by patients is a significant problem. I or other staff members occasionally encountered evidence of illegal drug use, which usually was ignored by the hospital's security personnel. On one occasion I learned that a patient had used a syringe to inject heroin into an IV bag. I was angry and disturbed, yet in view of the patient's addiction and social circumstances, I knew that there was little I could do to change such behavior.

Security personnel are reluctant to confront either the drug-using patients or the non-patient traffickers. Unless they actually witness a transaction, they claim that there is nothing they can do about the problem. On some occasions patients left the hospital to buy drugs. The lack of surprise on the part of physicians, nurses, or security personnel was remarkable. If a patient's "excursion" lasted too long, the nurses were authorized to strip the room and assign another patient to the bed. In the meantime, the patient's disappearance was reported to Security. If the nurse mentioned that the missing person was an AIDS patient, Security usually called off the search. Such patients usually returned via the emergency room anyway.

Ironically, the patients' experience with illegal drug use proves convenient from time to time. More than once I witnessed a doctor having difficulty giving an injection because the patient's veins had collapsed after years of drug abuse. Almost without fail the patient would say, "Let me do it, geez." In another context such episodes might have been humorous.

Drug addiction complicates the patient's prospects for recovery. Methadone and other substances counteract the licit prescriptions, sometimes further undermining the patient's physical condition. In addition, a variety of clinical and ethical issues pose barriers to the treatment of intravenous drug-using patients with AIDS. They include denial of an HIV-positive diagnosis coupled with denial of addiction; difficulty in coping with pain; familial conflict; continued substance abuse; and the need to coordinate social services. Both the patient and his or her family are often traumatized by the diagnosis, and the family may be reluctant to confront the patient's substance abuse.

Despite these obstacles, Barbara Faltz and Scott Madover note that:

> Crisis brought out by HIV+ or AIDS-related illness diagnosis may provide an opportunity to make a powerful intervention in the individual's substance abuse, and the patient's quality of life may improve as a result....For the individual troubled by the chaotic lifestyle that often accompanies drug or alcohol abuse, the crisis evoked by an AIDS diagnosis may generate a willingness to ask, 'What will I do with the rest of my life?' The patient may

choose either to get treatment for the abuse or to
continue it. Many do choose to 'Die High!'[1]

A barrier to treating intravenous drug-using patients with AIDS lies in the perspective and response of
caregivers. Moralistic attitudes toward drug and alcohol
abuse may lead caregivers to conclude that addicts would
stop if they really wanted to. This may prompt the
caregiver to take a lethargic, passive approach to serving
the patient. Moreover, if caregivers perceive drug or alcohol abuse to be a secondary problem of an emotional
nature rather than a primary condition, they may refer
patients to mental-health services rather than initiate
appropriate substance abuse treatment.

Caregivers appear to subscribe to an ideology as-
serting that a person must "hit rock bottom" before effective intervention can take place. They need to be re-
minded of the dynamics of addiction and the role of
motivation in recovery. If treatment is to be effective, it
is essential to understand the life of the drug user and
the power of the addiction. Drug use and related activities have become the focus of these patients' lives. The
drive to get drugs cannot be broken until other defi-
ciencies in their lives are addressed. Many of these individuals demonstrate very little knowledge about AIDS
and are unwilling to confront their risky behavior or come
to terms with the diagnosis. They want to deal only with
the immediate medical crisis. They have particular difficulty comprehending the correlation between factors in
their lifestyle and the disease. As a result, they tend not
to take medical advice very seriously.

Treatment Issues

At the beginning of my research I observed that few of
the HIV-positive or AIDS-diagnosed patients partici-

pated in treatment protocols. Specifically, AZT, the primary antiviral drug known to slow the growth of the HIV virus, was dispensed only sparingly to these patients. Aerosol pentamidine, a prophylactic used to treat PCP, was scarcely available for them. Toward the end of my study the hospital appeared to be using such treatments more aggressively. Still, not every AIDS patient was treated with AZT. Medical treatments were directed to the relief of specific symptoms or illnesses.

Medical follow-up for this population is limited. Little effort is made to ensure that patients comply with the prescribed regimen after they have been discharged. Customarily, patients using AZT are requested to see a physician every two weeks in order to have their white blood cell count checked. Patients complain that they cannot keep to such a schedule because the waiting lists at their neighborhood clinics do not allow for such stringent follow-up and the volume of other patients is such that they must wait for hours to see the health care provider.

A related issue is racial differences in the effectiveness of AIDS treatment.

> Since 1929, it has been established that there are substantial differences in how blacks and whites react to a given drug.... Black high blood pressure patients do not respond to the antihypertensive effects of Beta-blockers as well as white patients. Clearly, underrepresentation of blacks in hypertension clinical trials would lead to insufficient data to produce the kind of treatment best suited to both races.[2]

Thus, according to the *Journal of the American Medical Association,* in over half of the clinical trials where race was a factor, the percentage of black subjects was lower than the percentage of black residents in the area where the study was conducted.

Such disparities have prompted the National Institutes of Health to urge applicants for grants to include minorities in their studies. The Food and Drug Administration is also beginning to apply moral suasion in an attempt to make drug companies more sensitive to this issue. However, it is often difficult to persuade African-Americans and Hispanics to participate in clinical trials. Given the rather dubious history of treatment involving minorities, as well as the persistent rumor that AIDS is a laboratory-created form of germ warfare aimed at minorities, it is not surprising that members of minority groups are wary of both the trials and the clinicians.

Efforts to develop a vaccine for HIV and a cure for AIDS continue. Experimental drugs are in both the developmental and the trial stage. But again, blacks and Hispanics are a disproportionately small portion of the trial population. An increase in AIDS among the urban poor coupled with an inconsequential number of minority clinical subjects in drug trials could be disastrous. An HIV vaccine or AIDS cure might be found that works well for whites but is ineffective for blacks.

Taking clinical trials into minority communities may be awkward, but if representation of white males is disproportionately high, the drugs developed may not be best suited to the treatment of blacks and Hispanics or even safe for them in the long run.

AIDS and Public Health

It is an understatement to say that AIDS is a major public health problem; this cannot be stressed enough, particularly for women and children of color, who are increasingly and profoundly affected because of their marginal political and financial resources as well as ignorance and poor socialization. The Centers for Disease Control reports that as of July 1992 the average yearly cost of hospitalization for a person with AIDS was $38,300, and the cumulative cost by the end of 1995 is estimated to be $15.2 billion.

In the battle against AIDS, the scientific community has developed and tested numerous treatment options. Antivirals, such as Zidovudine (AZT), dideoxyinose (DDI), and dideoxycytidine (DDC), are designed to undermine the reproduction of HIV. DDI boosts T-4 cell counts, and DDC has the most potent anti-HIV effect of any nucleoside. Immune stimulators Naltrexone and gamma interferon, and stimulation of interleukin-2, which is already found in the body, are used to strengthen the immune system. Prophylaxis is designed to prevent opportunistic infections such as PCP.

Certain alternative treatments are more or less grudgingly accepted by the medical community, including acupuncture, massage therapy, psychological visualization, mediation, and nutritional therapy. These therapies, though relatively useful, are employed for a select population and not routinely made available or even discussed with the urban poor.

Since efforts to develop an AIDS vaccine have been unsuccessful, researchers are focusing on AIDS education and its impact on HIV prevention in ethnic minority communities. In *AIDS and IV Drug Abusers,* Don Des Jarlais notes that

> some of the most promising developments in limiting the spread of the Human Immunodeficiency Virus lie within the realm of health education. Such efforts undertaken by homosexual and bisexual communities...have led to reductions in self-reported high-risk sexual behaviors among sexually active homosexual and bisexual men as well as a reduction in the reported rates of other sexually transmitted diseases....AIDS education has become a growing concern among heterosexuals...being incorporated more often in sex education curricula

in the public schools. Despite these trends, AIDS education remains controversial. It is not yet widepread.[3]

AIDS education for intravenous drug users is even more complex. Because many of their activities are illegal and their political power base is nonexistent, measures to address the specific needs of this group have been limited.

A variety of vehicles are used to inform and educate the public about health issues. They include audiovisual media, newspapers and magazines, specialty pamphlets, direct mailings, and the schools. The language and style of such communications are designed to reach the greatest possible number of citizens—that is, mainstream America. Social and economic subgroups are not considered. It is not surprising, therefore, that members of these groups do not react or respond in large numbers to such messages, no matter how important.

At the onset of the AIDS epidemic, education programs were developed by and for gay white males. Despite the fact that the epidemic's demographic profile began to change in 1985, it is only very recently that education programs have been targeted toward the ethnic minority population. Even so, very few of those programs are developed by ethnic minority professionals. The significance of this fact cannot be overstated. The contrast in educational, social, and economic backgrounds between gay white males and members of ethnic minority groups calls for very different approaches to education. Comprehension of technical medical information is certainly an issue, but the cultural significance of "safe sex," condom use, bisexuality, homosexuality, and drug use is also important.

Because education is critical to controlling the spread of HIV and AIDS, the ability to reach across class boundaries is vital. Yet those who must design and provide this education sometimes have little knowledge of the culture or conditions of the poorest members of society.

The interviews conducted during my study suggest that the urban poor receive health education principally by word of mouth. Many of the patients learned about AIDS through community contacts and friends. Community-based outreach programs and clinics play an integral part in that communication channel. Community-based clinics and neighborhood hospitals are the major vehicles through which the poor receive medical care. Most of the patients had some experience with local clinics, but the vast majority received most of their medical care in hospital emergency rooms.

Several writers have noted obstacles to AIDS prevention efforts by community-based organizations. Chief among these is lack of resources—space, equipment, personnel, and money. These organizations are already overwhelmed. How can they possibly provide comprehensive AIDS education and services when they are unable to fulfill their current mission?

Current methods of reaching poor urban populations are ineffective in conveying the risk of AIDS infection and convincing these people that they are vulnerable. I interviewed too many individuals who did not believe that they were at risk for AIDS because they were not homosexual or did not "shoot" drugs. In particular, the women were under the misconception that people who have AIDS must "look sick" or be obviously, stereotypically homosexual. Even though some participants in my study had some awareness of the disease, their knowledge fell short, especially regarding factors that may influence the progression of the disease and about the types of treatment available. Also, it appears that some believe that a "magic bullet" will come along and provide a cure for AIDS.

The urban poor are passive in searching for and using information or resources with which to deal with the AIDS epidemic. They are totally dependent on the dominant society for whatever information or services are available for dealing with this crisis. In my opinion, public officials responsible for allocating funds for black and Latino community-based prevention initiatives must look for community organizations that have not only the technical expertise in medical aspects of AIDS but also credibility and the trust of the community.

Health Care For the Urban Poor

AIDS education efforts in minority communities highlight the poor health status of ethnic minority Americans, especially African-Americans. Most of the patients in my study lived in poverty. They lacked regular, gainful employment, permanent housing, proper nutrition, and family and community support. They experienced violence, crime, and other forms of physical or psychological abuse. Drug abuse was part of the fabric of their lives. Not all were direct participants in the drug "scene," but many were users. There was also a high level of alcoholism, and mental illness was not uncommon.

At the beginning of my research, the use of prophylaxis and neoplasms in the treatment of HIV infection and opportunistic AIDS infections was limited or nonexistent. Two and a half years later, prophylaxis, specifically antiretroviral drugs such as AZT, pentamidine (NebuPent and Pentam), and alpha interferon, was made available to these patients. During the first year of my observations, intravenous drug users were given antibiotics; few received AZT. None of the patients were included in ongoing clinical trials.

At present, patients who test positive for HIV are referred for clinical follow-up; that is, they are scheduled for further examination and possible initiation of treatment. If their T-4 cell count drops below 200, AZT and other prophylaxis-type treatments are prescribed. Patients with few family or community ties are not likely to comply with the treatment process because they receive little reinforcement and support during this stressful process.

Oremus Hospital claims to have developed a primary AIDS care model that takes an interdisciplinary approach to treatment. Despite this coordinated orientation, serious gaps remain in the provision of service and treatment. The health care workers do not always cooperate with one another. Class and cultural barriers limit communication among the various caregivers. In general, the staff has a negative perception of the patients. I observed a certain degree of professional lethargy among staff members who had held their jobs for so long, had seen so much, and were so close to retirement that they went about their duties like automatons, doing only what was required to remain employed.

In *Illness as Metaphor,* Susan Sontag writes about the "mythologizing" of diseases, especially those of unknown etiology. She comments that such illnesses take on a symbolic meaning when the origin and causes are mysterious and unclear. Her thoughts are particularly relevant in the cases examined in this book. When AIDS was first identified, it was connected to the nation's gay community. Reports of a strange new illness and the revelation that many of its victims were homosexual led to its being named GRID—Gay Related Immune Disorder. Sontag writes:

Nothing is more punitive than to give a disease a meaning—that meaning being a moralistic one. Any disease whose causality is murky, and for which treatment is ineffective tends to be awash in significance....Feelings about evil are projected onto a disease [so enriched with meaning] it is projected onto the world....Patients who are instructed that they have unwittingly caused their disease are being made to feel that they deserved it.[4]

Still, more than thirteen years into the epidemic,

some people seem to believe that they are at no risk of contracting an AIDS-related illness, that the "AIDS thing" is a disease of gay men and drug addicts. Many people see HIV infection and AIDS as the consequences of unnatural or antisocial behavior. Some even go so far as to say that "they get what they deserve." There is some doubt, therefore, that the American people and the U.S. government are truly committed to coping with and ultimately discovering a cure for AIDS.

In April 1990 an article in the *New York Times* noted that

> The Federal Government's top advisory panel on AIDS policy [the National Commission on AIDS] told President Bush...that AIDS policy in the U.S. was like an orchestra without a conductor, because the Government had failed to lead the campaign against the epidemic effectively. All across the country there is a cry for leadership from the Federal Government and partnership between the various levels of government.[4]

Among the panel's recommendations were: the establishment of a cabinet level post to be held by an official commissioned to devise a national strategy to cope with AIDS; provision of disaster relief for the areas hardest hit by the epidemic; enactment of antidiscrimination legislation to protect people with AIDS; and the elimination of government restrictions on the content of AIDS educational brochures. Five years later there has been no effort to meet these goals.

Notes

1. Barbara G. Faltz and Scott Madover, "Treatment of Substance Abuse in Patients with HIV Infection," in Larry Siegel, ed., *AIDS and Substance Abuse* (New York: Haworth Press, 1988), p. 145.

2. Robert Santiago, "Drug Trials and Race," in Angela Mitchell, "AIDS: We Are Not Immune," *Emerge: Our Voice in Today's World*, November 1990, p. 35.

3. Don C. Des Jarlais, "Foreword," in Robert P. Galea, Benjamin F. Lewis, and Lori A. Baker, eds., *AIDS and IV Drug Abusers* (Owings Mills, MD: National Health Publishing, 1988), p. xvii.

4. Philip J. Hilts, "Panel Says Government Is Not Leading the AIDS Fight," *New York Times*, April 25, 1990, pp. A1, A17.

8

The Caseworker

THE first day I entered Oremus Hospital I was shown the medical ward where I would spend the next twenty-two months. I met five patients in various stages of HIV diagnosis and AIDS-related illness. I wondered what I had gotten myself into. At first I was overwhelmed by the suffering I witnessed. During those early days I would have to leave the room in the middle of a counseling session in order to regain my composure. There were many sleepless nights as my rest was invaded by memories of patients moaning, complaining, and physically struggling with illness and death.

I didn't want to be there. I felt astonished, saddened, heartbroken at the magnitude of the illness there. I hated the sight and smell of people so distorted by disease. They moved so slowly, and the look of death was in their eyes. Some of them would not talk to me.

In time the initial shock dissipated and I focused more on my duties and responsibilities as a caseworker. After gathering the necessary demographic information and family history for the case record, I assessed each patient's social service needs and helped develop a hospital discharge plan for that patient. This required interaction with the patient and assessment of his or her understanding of the diagnosis or medical condition. This was not usually an easy process. It often took a long time to engage patients in conversation. Questions about matters of lifestyle were often perceived as invasions of privacy and viewed with great suspicion. It became clear that I needed to find ways of establishing trust and confidence with people whose lives were often characterized by desertion, betrayal, and dishonesty.

During the initial meetings it was not uncommon for patients to refuse to speak with me ("What the fuck do you want?" "Who are you?" "I don't want to be answering so many questions!"). Some people ignored me, simply pulling the sheets over their heads and hoping that I would leave the room. If they spoke, it was to ask that I turn off the lights and close the door on my way out. When I reached the point where I no longer took such rejections personally, I would take a seat, remain silent, and wait until the patient spoke. This approach often required several tries to be effective. Other times, I attempted to buy the patients' confidence by doing little favors for them—purchasing cigarettes, candy, or clothing or making telephone calls, sometimes taking their requests to the doctors or nurses. Reports of these actions circulated among the patients, and over time I cultivated a favorable reputation ("That Ayala is OK, you can talk to him, he listens...respects our type of people").

As a caseworker, I was exposed to the factors that these patients dealt with on a regular basis: homelessness, drug addiction, loneliness, chaotic lifestyles, and now the unfamiliar routine of hospitalization and the uncontrollable developments occurring in their bodies. Much of my counseling time was spent encouraging the patients to speak about their lives and their understanding of AIDS. It was important for me to be genuine, empathic, and honest about caring for them and wanting to make their hospital experience easier. Since most were homeless, intravenous drug users, sex workers, criminals of various kinds, or homosexuals, and sometimes various combinations of these, they were unaccustomed to sharing their experiences with anyone who listened in a

nonjudgmental fashion. Even if they believed that I was
there to help, they were often curious about my mo-
tives. I always told them that I was a caseworker; sometimes I mentioned that I was a graduate student in sociology.

There is a thin line between empathy and
overidentification, and being "tested" by patients clari-
fied this issue for me. I was always at risk of being used
by patients or manipulated into actions that could sometimes prove harmful to them in the long run. This was
particularly true of the substance abusers, who routinely
tried to badger, beg, or cajole me into obtaining larger
doses of methadone for them. At first I would rush to
the nurses' station in order to accommodate the patient.
Fortunately, the more experienced members of the staff
and certain situations involving individual patients helped
me realize that the patients' behavior was manipulative
and reflected poor impulse control or pain intolerance
rather than genuine need. Moreover, my lack of experience in this area created friction with the medical staff.
Some of the doctors and nurses perceived my intervention on behalf of patients as an attempt to impose my
judgment on theirs.

The patients had great difficulty coping with the
emotions surrounding their fears of the illness and their
mortality. The counseling sessions were often intense and
physically draining, and as I was both caseworker and
researcher, they required a serious commitment of time
and energy. Being available both physically and emotionally to the patients and their families was challenging; it
was also a spiritual awakening. It became clear that it
would be necessary, indeed unavoidable, for me to reflect on the issues of death and dying if I was to provide
any assistance to patients going through the dying process. Crossing the line from caseworker to fellow human
being and back became less mechanical with each encounter.

Because the number of patients exceeded the capacity and resources of the hospital and neighborhood social services, I was in a state of continual frustration. I felt that my efforts were useless in the face of the patients' deteriorating health and imminent death. The magnitude of their psychosocial, medical, and financial needs, and their lack of political power, brought to the landscape of my interaction a sense of helplessness. Simply knowing that my "shift" would soon be finished was a help. At other times absenteeism was the only way I could cope with my anger and depression. As time went by I had to make a concerted, conscious effort to distance myself emotionally from the patients' pain in order to minimize my own. Objectivity was the only way to deliver the best possible service at the lowest personal cost.

   After a discussion with a fellow social worker I wrote the following notes:

> On this ward I deal with twenty-eight patients. It's difficult. I have to document everything that I'm doing with them. Hey, we're short-staffed; could you imagine trying to be on top of the histories and personal circumstances of every one of these patients? I mean, this one is homeless, that one is a drug addict, the other one has AIDS and won't face it. You have the doctors always pushing you to find housing for patients...they want them OUT. So they see you in the halls and yell, 'Hey, did you find housing for so and so?' We're just so short-staffed; sometimes I just can't handle this. I don't know how I do this.

> Boy, so many people are dying up here, it's like a dying club. Sometimes I can't believe it. I just need to get out of here. I'm transferring to the ER. At least in there the patients keep moving; they come in and move out.

Eventually I found that I needed to make mental notes of the specific ways in which I helped each patient in order to feel good about the job. I focused on simply being present, listening, providing emotional support, and touching patients as concrete ways of easing their pain and fear of death. Acknowledging the validity of their lives, encouraging them to cease dwelling on the past and live each day as best they could was difficult, but it was essential, both to their well-being and to mine. I made a point of observing demonstrations of commitment, even heroism on the part of co-workers. It was important to celebrate the fact the the "glass was half full" rather than "half empty."

Time proved to be a finite resource. I was never sure that there would be enough of it to uncover the needed research information or adequately serve each patient's needs. It was not uncommon for a patient to become incapacitated or to die with my work unfinished. I could not help those patients verbalize their understanding of the diagnosis, finalize discharge plans, or arrange for their last meetings with their families.

My increasing weariness and occasional depression forced me to dissociate myself emotionally from the job from time to time. I concentrated on being more professional in the execution of my duties. I became more savvy to the maneuvering of "hustlers" disguising their requests as real expressions of need. Growing to understand the background and nature of the patients enabled me to distinguish a patient participating in a bona fide Methadone program from one who simply wanted the drug.

The issue of drug addiction has special implications for caseworkers. There is poor communication and, hence, little cooperation between drug treatment facilities, community-based organizations, and the hospital. It is difficult to discern what type of care is provided to patients both before and after hospitalization. Certain information cannot be obtained from other facilities because it is held as confidential either by custom or under the law. Caseworkers therefore have to rely on the patients for information, and their lack of knowledge and communication skills makes it difficult to provide comprehensive medical or social services. The fact that patients frequently move from one clinic, drug treatment program, or hospital to another heightens the confusion and results in fragmented, sporadic care.

Social workers are called upon to convince patients to be more cooperative. This may be accomplished by increasing their understanding of their medical condition while addressing the myriad social conditions affecting their lives. The social worker takes on the role of advocate for the patient, attempting to sensitize physicians and nurses to the nonmedical issues affecting the patient's life. Although the social worker gains the trust and cooperation of the patient, the doctor-patient relationship does not necessarily improve. To some extent, an adversary relationship—"us versus them"—develops between the staff and the patients.

The attitudes of staff members at Oremus Hospital were condescending at times. They tended to "blame the victim," believing that the patients' illness was their own fault ("If they didn't do what they're doing, they wouldn't have AIDS. If they'd follow my directions, they'd be outta here!"). They also had a poor attitude toward the caseworker. Such attitudes were expressed when a doctor would interrupt a counseling session, discounting my presence and invalidating my work, sometimes acting as if I wasn't even there. One intern interrupted a session and instructed me not to allow the patient to cry and "get out of control." He insisted that I focus on helping the patient understand the medical procedure and the diagnosis. Ironically, I was doing just that, but with his clinical blinders on he was unable to see that the expression of emotion could serve as a means of attaining greater understanding. Another incident occurred at a time when a patient was near death. As I held her hand and attempted to reassure and comfort her as she passed through this most fearful of moments, a doctor abruptly came in to draw blood. Despite his awareness of the patient's condition, he could not separate himself from his clinical routine even for a moment.

Despite the negative attitudes of some staff members, I was usually able to convince them of the need for more attention for patients who were truly in need. I learned how to approach the staff with unusual requests. I also learned to respect the staff's work habits and accept the fact that they are the ones who decide when patients will be seen and which medical treatments they will receive.

Conversely, the physicians and nurses relied on me to identify the patients' social service needs. It was my function to clarify the medical issues for the patient and his or her family, if any. I was responsible for the development and implementation of discharge plans so as to avoid unnecessarily long hospital stays. In the best of circumstances, this proved advantageous for both the patient and the hospital. But in too many cases the lack of appropriate housing, supportive counseling, community-based referrals, or other services would leave patients to fend for themselves once they were discharged from the hospital.

Discharge proved especially difficult for the homeless patients. Patients with confirmed AIDS diagnoses were not accepted by local shelters. This was a source of considerable friction between the hospital administrators and doctors and the caseworkers and neighborhood social service organizations. Battles over turf or areas of professional responsibility could easily leave patients without adequate care.

I was able to contain my fear of exposure by keeping in mind the information circulated by the CDC about modes of HIV transmission. I was more concerned about susceptibility to airborne bacteria expelled by patients with rare, more or less contagious diseases such as salmonella, tuberculosis, meningitis, chicken pox, and herpes simplex. Complicating the issue further was the observation that neither the patients nor the staff always abided by established precautionary guidelines. I began to fear contagion from less-than-vigilant co-workers. I took precautions, but the more time I spent at the hospital, the more concerned I became about the possibility of infection.

In the end, the need to continue my work overshadowed my fear of contagion. The patients needed someone to serve as a link between their desolate existence and people who could provide some comfort. Even the health care workers, however entrenched they were in medical procedures, continued to serve. Perhaps one can assume that they did so merely to maintain their livelihood. But when nurses come in day after day and don protective clothing, caring for patient after patient, one cannot dismiss the knowledge that they feel the pangs of humanity and do their jobs because they experience the rewards of merging medical treatment with human understanding.

EPILOGUE

NOT long ago I was standing near one of the nurses' stations at Oremus Hospital. A nurse asked me if I had heard about Joseph's death. Joseph had been a physician assistant at the hospital. "He died of AIDS," she told me. "What an unfortunate thing. I'm so shocked. He was so intelligent; he really took care of the patients..." Another nurse interrupted, saying "If he was so intelligent, why did he get AIDS?" A third said, "Look, I never questioned his lifestyle; you know that Joseph was so private. Hey, let's say that you're in love with someone. Do you think you would always wear a condom each time you have sex?" She noted that she was a professional and aware of HIV transmission, yet she sometimes did not require that her partner use a condom.

Another nurse talked about how she had noticed that something was wrong with Joseph. She had observed that he was losing weight, had rashes on his face, and looked tired all the time; "sometimes he even looked like some of the patients." She said she had felt that something was wrong but had been afraid to ask questions.

I knew Joseph. He had confided in me that he was HIV-positive, and we had talked about his plans. He did not want me to tell anyone on the staff because they would talk about him and would want to know how he had become infected. He also feared that his co-workers would ask questions about his sexuality and might even shun him, as he had heard their remarks about some of the patients with AIDS. He said that he hoped to go out on disability before the gossip started.

As I stood there listening to the nurses, I felt angry that even in a hospital we couldn't get beyond the stereotypes and stigma surrounding AIDS. I retreated into my own silence, thinking about how right Joseph had been. It was only after his death that people began to talk, to understand, to break the silence. And then I thought about my friend Bill, who died of AIDS ten years ago. All these years have passed, and AIDS still holds us in a grip of silence and fear. Our judgment and compassion are continually tested and our humanity questioned as we struggle to understanding the suffering of AIDS.

Index

acceptance, in dying process, 80, 86–87
Accreditation Council on Graduate Medical Education, 24
AIDS, 9
    disclosure of, 3, 63, 64, 94
    incidence of, 11–12, 13, 15
        in African-Americans, 11–12, 15
        in Hispanic Americans, 12, 15
        in homosexuals, 11, 105
        in intravenous drug users, 13
    perceptions of, 36–38, 105–6
    and poverty, 14–16, 104–5
    and public health, 100–105
        medical treatments, 101, 104
    silence surrounding, 1, 2, 90–92, 118
    stigma of, 2, 3, 8, 28, 42, 46–47, 67, 83, 118
    transmission of, 5, 6, 10, 11, 37, 38
        risk factors in, 12–14
    and women, 13–14, 72–74, 75
AIDS and IV Drug Abusers (Des Jarlais), 101
AIDS dementia complex, 10, 52
AIDS education, 15–16, 101–4
    community-based outreach programs, 103–4
    and ethnic minorities, 102, 104
    and homosexuals, 102
    and intravenous drug users, 102
AIDS Hotline, 2, 3

109, 114, 119
admission policies of, 25–26, 28–29
AIDS care model, 105
overidentification, by caseworker, 111

"passive poor," 14
PCP. *See* pneumocystis Carinii pneumonia
Pentam, 104
pentamidine, 99, 104
pneumocystis Carinii pneumonia (PCP), 10, 99, 101
privacy, 94, 110
prophylaxis, 2, 101, 105
prostitution, and transmission of AIDS, 5, 6, 73

religion, and acceptance of death, 87
resuscitation, 46, 61
risk factors in transmission of AIDS, 13–14, 16

"safe sex," 11, 102, 117
"San Francisco Model" of health care organizations, 11
Santiago, Robert, 107*n*
Selik, A. M., 17*n*
Sontag, Susan, 105
substance abuse, 104, 110
    and denial of death, 81
    detoxification/rehabilitation, 35, 96
    and disclosure of HIV status, 71
    implications for caseworkers, 113–14
    and incidence of AIDS, 13
    policy issues related to, 93, 95–98
    and relations with family members, 69–72
    staff reaction, 59
    and transmission of AIDS, 5, 6, 7, 12, 73–74
suicide, 85–86
Supplemental Security Insurance (SSI), 30

T-4 lymphocytes, 9, 101, 104
toxoplasmosis, 10, 69